Pet Heroes

Pet Heroes

PAUL SIMONS

ORION

Copyright © 1996 Paul Simons

All rights reserved

The right of Paul Simons to be identified as the author of this work has
been asserted by him in accordance with the
Copyright, Designs and Patents Act 1988.

First published in Great Britain in 1996 by
Orion
An imprint of Orion Books Ltd
Orion House, 5 Upper St Martin's Lane, London WC2H 9EA

A CIP catalogue record for this book is available
from the British Library

ISBN 0 75280 738 2

Filmset by Selwood Systems, Midsomer Norton
Printed in Great Britain by
Butler & Tanner Ltd, Frome and London

CONTENTS

INTRODUCTION

Pets are companions, friends, guardians – in fact so much a part of our lives that we tend to take them for granted. But there are hidden depths to pets that we rarely appreciate, which are sometimes only revealed in astonishing acts of heroism. Thanks to their intelligence, loyalty and powerful sense of smell and hearing, pets have saved countless human lives.

Pet Heroes is about extraordinary feats of heroism performed by ordinary pets. It illustrates the enormous range of pet heroism and some of the mysteries surrounding this subject. There are pets that have saved their owners from mortal danger, like the terrier that came to the rescue of her owner in a diabetic coma by fetching her a bag of jelly babies, tipping them onto the floor and then nuzzling her head to rouse her. Or the cat called Samantha who helped save forty-four people from an apartment-block fire in California. And then there's Ben, a family Labrador, who rescued his owner's four-month-old baby from an abductor.

Pets can also warn their owners of serious medical conditions well before any human realises the danger. Dogs have detected skin cancers, the onset of diabetic comas and epileptic fits perhaps all by smell, and cats seem to have an amazing sense of imminent death, enabling them to raise the alarm, but we don't understand how they do it.

Pets have also rescued other animals. Tarka, a Labrador, dived into a fast-flowing river to rescue a drowning terrier. Scarlett the cat repeatedly ran into a blazing house in New York to rescue her five kittens. And when a pigsty caught fire in Massachusetts, a mother hog suffered burns while rescuing her piglets from the flames.

Many pets have shown undying loyalty to their owners, even after the owner's death. Greyfriars Bobby was a dog so attached to his deceased master that he visited his grave daily for fourteen years until he died himself. He became such a folkhero that his home city of Edinburgh dedicated a monument in his honour. This sort of devotion is not only confined to dogs – bees have been known to pay their last respects to their deceased keepers.

The powers of navigation of pets have astounded scientists. A cat in America walked 2,500 miles home after his owners moved house. Racing pigeons regularly fly hundreds of miles in all weathers back to their home loft, and dogs have been known to return home by catching buses or trains on their own!

Animals' powerful sense of smell has led to some amazing dramas. Eire's top sniffer dog was so successful at finding heroin he was kidnapped by drug barons and nearly executed on their orders before being rescued. A mongrel called Pickles became world famous when he sniffed a hedge in a suburb of London and discovered the solid gold World Cup for soccer which had been stolen and abandoned there. A dog on the Isle of Wight bit off more than he could chew when he dug up one of the largest dinosaur bones ever found.

Animals have withstood unbelievable tests of endurance. Floss the sheepdog fell over the edge of a cliff, but survived for two weeks on a ledge below in blizzard conditions without food or water. A three-year-old tabby cat travelled 300,000 miles after becoming lost inside a jumbo jet's rear ceiling panel. Sandy, a mongrel and a British army mascot in Egypt, was captured by Germans during the Second World War but escaped and walked back to his base in Alexandria across 140 miles of desert.

Pets have been the unspoken heroes of wars. They ran messages, laid telephone cables along war fronts, led and guarded soldiers behind enemy lines, tracked down buried bodies, bombs and mines, carried munitions and searched out wounded soldiers. Some of them have been honoured with awards as high as the Victoria Cross and presented before presidents.

Throughout the Second World War Blitz sniffer dogs were used to track down buried survivors, even though at the outbreak of war the civil defence authorities were unconvinced that dogs would be

Rob the parachuting collie led the SAS on desperate missions behind enemy lines in the Second World War, becoming the most decorated animal in British history, with eight medals. (Imperial War Museum)

useful. Irma, an Alsatian sniffer dog, won the highest animal honour for valour for locating a record total of 191 buried people, twenty-one of whom were alive (her picture is on page 109). Rob the Paradog made over twenty solo parachute drops into North Africa and Italy with SAS units inside enemy territory. Decorated eight times, he was probably the most honoured animal in British history, his awards including two Victoria Crosses for leading soldiers back to safety after commando missions and rescuing escaped prisoners of war. Pigeons were used for flying messages over hundreds of miles often under dangerous conditions, from secret agents inside enemy territory, aircraft crews forced to ditch in hostile territory, and resistance groups.

Simon, the only cat to receive the prestigious Dickin Medal, survived burns and shrapnel wounds during an intense bombardment on board HMS *Amethyst* during the Chinese Civil War, but still carried on his duties, which were catching rats and raising the morale of his crew during a three months' blockade.

Perhaps most sensational of all, many owners claim their pets can anticipate their actions telepathically and know exactly when they are due to arrive home. Pets have also had premonitions of disasters, such as hurricanes and earthquakes, and have raised the alarm and saved lives. These mysterious powers of pets go beyond their senses of smell or hearing and need serious investigation.

Pets have made their own modest heroic impact in normal daily life, benefiting their owners in tangible ways. Scientific studies show that pets often reduce stress in their owners and can improve overall wellbeing and sociability. This is probably why pets have been used very successfully to assist patients' recovery in hospital, and to help the blind, deaf or disabled, disturbed children and the mentally ill. It seems that we have a need for animal companionship, and they do us the world of good.

How do they do it? A cat's or dog's sense of smell is at least forty times more powerful than a human's. Their odour-sensing cells are lined up inside the membrane of the nose. A German shepherd dog's nose, for example, contains over 220 million smell sensor cells, which is why their noses tend to be long. Another characteristic of cats and dogs is their acute hearing: they are able to register

Cats are brave, too. For three appalling months in the Chinese Civil War, Simon kept up the morale of his besieged ship HMS Amethyst *despite suffering injuries from an artillery attack.* (Imperial War Museum)

frequencies as high as 35,000 cycles per second, compared to an upper limit of about 20,000 cycles per second for humans, and they can distinguish minute differences in tone that go unnoticed by the human ear. Dogs also have an inner ear they can shut off, helping them to filter out general background noise. Cats and dogs also have far superior night vision, thanks partly to the reflective layer at the back of the eye, which effectively gives them two chances to capture the same image.

But they seem to have other senses we've yet to recognise. They may have a sense of magnetism, which gives them an inbuilt compass to navigate by. They could also have a pressure sensor. This behaves like a barometer and tells them about changes in the weather. Yet some stories of pet heroism are so incredible that they defy belief unless we accept some mystical power at work – what has been called an animal's 'sixth sense', or a type of extrasensory perception (ESP) or telepathy. This is a highly controversial field, poorly studied by science, but there are strikingly similar patterns across many of these stories giving them added credibility. What emerges are aspects of animal behaviour that are rarely discussed in science textbooks and are difficult to explain. Eventually, in the light of these events, we may have to change our views on animal senses and behaviour.

However, powerful or mysterious senses alone aren't enough to explain our pet heroics. They are obviously brave animals and often risk their lives to save another life. It's also clear that pet heroes show considerable intelligence and don't just follow their instinctive reflexes, like panicking in a fire or running from a violent beast. They recognise a crisis, take emergency action and often have to solve difficult problems, like the rottweiler that couldn't wake up his owners in a fire so he rang the doorbell. But are they intelligent and do they think like us? They probably don't have a conscience which lets them think of abstracts like what they're going to do the next day. But they do have mental powers we sorely underestimate. Pets are acute observers of us and the rest of their world and can memorise things in minute detail, so they recognise anything out of the ordinary. This talent makes them extraordinarily alert to danger and helps explain many different sorts of pet hero behaviour.

Yet how much they use their own instinct is difficult to know and depends to some extent on the history of pet evolution. Dogs were first domesticated from wolves by prehistoric people for hunting about 12,000 years ago, after the last ice age. Some dog behaviour still owes much to their wolf pack heritage, which is why they develop such strong loyalties to their owners. But in the course of breeding, different characteristics have been developed. Terriers were bred for hunting vermin, hounds for larger prey, collies for working with farm animals, and so on. Some breeds are naturally cleverer than others, others braver, more aggressive, more playful, for example.

Cats were domesticated later than dogs, about 4,000 years ago in ancient Egypt, which is partly why they are far more independent. Also, their wild cat ancestors were less sociable than wolves, and this may explain why there are far fewer cat heroes than dog heroes.

Throughout *Pet Heroes* I've tried to feature only volunteer heroes, which means excluding animals trained for a purpose, such as police dogs and dogs for the blind. However, in the chapter on war and pets I've included stories about pets donated for military service and trained for a purpose, which were often returned to civilian life as pets afterwards. I have also included a few cases of heroic farm animals. You won't find many horse heroes, however, because most acts of equine bravery have been performed by 'professional' horses in the police or the army.

Although based in Britain, stories are featured from all over the world, and include examples from the United States, Canada, France, Germany, Italy, Japan, South Africa, Australia and New Zealand. Pet heroes are by no means exclusively British!

I hope you come away looking at pets with new eyes, as creatures capable of extraordinary bravery, possessing powers we have hardly begun to understand. The humble animals that share millions of peoples' lives can be, in fact, very special creatures.

I

Pets to the Rescue

FOUR-LEGGED FIRE ALARMS

Fire is a universal threat to life that all animals recognise instantly, and because they have an acute sense of smell they usually raise the alarm while their owners are still sleeping peacefully. Pets saving their owners' lives from fire, sometimes at enormous risk to themselves, is by far the most common feat of heroism. Many of these heroes have been awarded medals for bravery. But what makes these acts of heroism so intriguing is that in the face of extreme danger, animals show not only courage but also considerable intelligence and ingenuity in attempting to alert their owners.

ROC

On the night of 27 June 1996 a violent thunderstorm raged over Bern in North Carolina, and Rosevelt and Linda Mathews woke up in the small hours to the sound of their rottweiler, Roc, barking fit to bust in the back garden. They thought he was simply frightened of the storm and ignored him. Then the front doorbell started ringing over and over again. They went downstairs and opened the door – to find Roc jumping up and ringing the bell. He had never been taught this trick, but he must have known that this was the only way to attract his owners' attention. When the Mathews went outside to investigate they discovered the roof of their house ablaze.

It had been hit by lightning. They evacuated their two children before the house burnt down completely. Roc had saved their lives. Rottweilers are highly intelligent dogs, particularly good at problem-solving and with good memories. So when Roc was faced with his home burning down and barking got him nowhere, he must have realised that a doorbell was the ideal way to get his owners' attention, although he had never used it before.

HARVEY

Harvey, a basset hound, was quietly snoozing in his kitchen when smoke started curling under the door. Normally he slept in the bedroom, but his owner, Sandra Kramer, was ill with flu. Harvey didn't hesitate. He went berserk, knocking over the kitchen stools, howling, barking and crashing about to rouse Sandra and her five-year-old daughter Leah. By the time Sandra woke up, her bedroom and her daughter's room were full of smoke. With Harvey by their side, they ran out of the house, where Sandra used her portable phone to summon the fire brigade. But Harvey hadn't finished his rescue work yet. When the firemen entered the house, he went in with them and reappeared a few moments later followed by the family cat. 'I'd been worrying about the cat because I couldn't find her,' explained Sandra. 'Harvey was showing the firemen where to go.' Harvey's heroism was an excellent example of a dog originally bred for hunting with a keen sense of smell that alerted him to the smoke. But by rescuing the family cat he also showed great courage and loyalty to another species of animal, which is not usually expected from basset hounds.

BRUCE

Fire has produced many other astonishing acts of heroism by pets. In 1937, an apartment block in Boston caught fire and newspapers of the time reported a blind man being led to safety by his sheepdog Bruce. One of the other survivors was a woman with two small children. She tried to run back into the blazing building, screaming that her baby was trapped inside, but firemen stopped her. Bruce's master urged him in and two minutes later he emerged, coat aflame, suffering burns and having lost an eye, but with the baby alive and unhurt, hanging by its nightgown from his teeth. Originally sheepdogs were bred for herding farm animals, and Bruce showed these instincts in rescuing the baby. But he also demonstrated extraordinary courage in running through the flames and suffering great pain.

SAMANTHA

Perhaps the world record for numbers of human lives saved by a pet belongs to Samantha, a black Burmese cat from Rancho Mirage, California. On the night of 13 April 1976, her owners, Francesca and Robert Galbraith, were asleep in their apartment, when Samantha became unusually agitated and began pouncing on the couple's bed, miaowing insistently. 'She even began using her teeth to pull back the sheet,' Mrs Galbraith told reporters afterwards. The couple awoke to find smoke filling the bedroom. Mrs Galbraith rang the fire brigade and then ran through the apartment block banging on doors to wake her neighbours. A fire which had started in the building's basement storeroom had taken hold and was sweeping up through the block. Samantha's alarm call had saved the lives of forty-four residents. Samantha became a national hero and was awarded the American Humane Association's prestigious William O. Stillman Award for Animal Bravery. Her achievement also demonstrated the powerful sense of smell which all cats have and how clever they can be – she had to use all her ingenuity to get her owners' attention.

SULTAN

Apart from fire, pets have saved their owners from all sorts of other domestic dangers. Sultan, a four-year-old German shepherd dog prevented his owner from being electrocuted. On New Year's Day 1994, Alex Flemming of Bloemfontein, South Africa was extending the electric cable of his vacuum cleaner to clean the inside of his car, when he was thrown on to his back by a severe electric shock. He began rapidly to lose consciousness. Sultan, sensing the peril to his owner, reacted immediately by pulling the cable away from Mr Flemming's body, thereby saving his life. Sultan suffered severe burns to his mouth but recovered fully after veterinary treatment. He was awarded a gold medal for bravery by the South African Society for the Prevention of Cruelty to Animals. German shepherd dogs are famous for their intelligence – Sultan realised what caused his master to collapse and then showed great bravery in tackling the live cable.

* * *

DANGEROUS LEAKS

ELLIOTT

Dogs and cats are usually, but not exclusively, the best guardians. Elliott, a blue-fronted Amazon parrot, saved the lives of the Ascolillo family of East Boston one night in 1987. Elliott's uncharacteristic squawking and thrashing awakened the Ascolillos in time to escape the toxic fumes which had poured into their home from a neighbourhood gas leak. In fact, Elliott demonstrated the acute sense of smell all birds have, which is why canaries were once used by coal miners for detecting gas leaks.

RINGO

During the spring and early summer of 1995, Carol and Ray Steiner from Bowling Green in Wood County, Massachusetts became progressively ill with headaches, high blood pressure, memory loss and lethargy. Then early one August morning in 1995 their red tabby, Ringo, woke them up in a blind panic. 'Ringo started throwing himself against the front door, then the rear door of our house,' said Carol. When she let him outdoors Ringo turned round as if to tell Carol to follow him. He led her to the back of the house. He began digging amongst the jagged rocks there, which is not something a cat would typically do, and Carol smelled a strong gas leak from a buried pipeline. The gas had drifted indoors and made them feel ill. Once the pipe was repaired their symptoms disappeared. Ringo had used outstanding intelligence to lead his owners to the cause of the problem and he was awarded the American Humane Association's William O. Stillman Award for Animal Bravery, becoming one of only ten cats to win the award in its hundred year history. His picture appears on the back of the jacket of this book.

SNORT

Birds and cats aren't the only animals to raise the alarm about gas leaks. A female potbellied pig called Snort saved her owners, Deborah and Collin Stolpe, from a potentially deadly gas leak on board the bus they were living in. One bitter cold night in Colorado in November 1995, the Stolpes were sleeping in their bus, which was kept warm by a propane heater, when the normally mellow Snort started oinking and running through the bus in great distress. Deborah got up three times to take the pig out, but each time Snort wanted to stay inside although she remained restless. Then Deborah tried waking her husband, but he suddenly starting having convulsions, which she interpreted as a heart attack. The nightmare grew worse when she tried to call for an ambulance and found her own speech was slurred and her vision hazy. In fact, they were both suffering from carbon monoxide poisoning caused by a leak from the heater, and Snort was trying to warn them about the gas. Had Snort not made such a commotion in the bus and refused to go outside where she would have been safe, it is likely the Stolpes would have died. Snort was the first pig ever to receive a life-saving award from the American Humane Association. She illustrated that pigs are highly intelligent, loyal characters, and can make outstanding pets.

* * *

HEROICS IN THE WATER

Pets have saved many humans from drowning, often putting their own lives at risk in rivers, ponds, seas and freezing waters. By far

*Who says pigs aren't smart? Snort, a pet potbellied pig, saved her owners'
lives from a deadly gas leak by frantically oinking and running indoors,
despite the grave danger to herself.* (American Humane Association)

the best lifesavers – but not exclusively – have been dogs, and on occasion they have saved complete strangers. This cavalier disregard for their own safety tells a lot about the bravery and loyalty dogs feel towards all humans. Perhaps this comes from a deep instinct dating back to their origins as wolves, when members of the pack saved each other from danger. As pets, dogs have transferred that loyalty to humans, and especially their owners whom they see as the leader of their pack.

HENKA

On 30 May 1996, two-year-old Rhys Loram of Stowmarket in Suffolk insisted on playing one last game with the family dog Henka before going to bed, and they went outside together into the garden. A short while later Rhys's mother Joanne heard the German shepherd dog going wild. She rushed into the garden and found Rhys face down in the fish pond, his head and shoulders trapped beneath a metal grid cover in eighteen inches of water. Henka was pawing at the little boy as he lay with his legs in the air. 'I ran outside expecting that the dog had hurt himself, only to see Rhys in the water. Henka was frantic and trying to pull him out,' Joanne said. She scooped up her son, who opened his eyes, coughed up some water and later fully recovered, but if Henka hadn't raised the alarm it would have been a different story.

ZIGGY AND STELLA

Australian Women's Weekly reported a story of such superb co-ordi-nation between a pair of dogs it shows either that dogs have far better powers of communication than we suspect or that some dogs are telepathic.

In 1994, border collie Ziggy and rottweiler Stella teamed up to save their master Chris Georgiou from drowning. Chris was out on his farm on a cold September afternoon in the Adelaide Hills in Australia. By 5p.m. he was tired, having spent three hours cutting wild lilies from the banks of his trout lake. Clutching an iron rail in order to pull himself clear of the muddy bank, he accidentally banged his head against it, stunning himself. He lost his grip and slid into the icy water and because he could not swim he felt a rush of terror. He clawed madly at the slippery bank but he was heavily weighed down with overalls, a thick jumper, coat and gumboots and couldn't get a grip. 'The dam was four metres deep and I was just thinking, I'm gone,' Chris said. 'My wife was overseas. There was nobody else around.'

But faithful Ziggy was on the bank. 'I could see him running back and forth. He was making a hell of a noise,' said Chris. 'It wasn't a bark but an unusual sort of cry. I'd never heard anything like it before.' A moment later, getting close to his last breath, Chris felt a touch on his shoulder. It was Stella, his other dog who had waded in. 'I hadn't seen her since lunchtime when I'd left her at the house. She's a lazy dog and she'd been asleep in her kennel!'

She had dived straight into the water and swum to reach Chris. Stella was a large dog, weighing about fifty-six kilograms, and Chris managed to get an arm around her body and haul himself a few metres away to where he knew there was a big log just below the water's surface. 'I still don't know if I steered the dog towards it or the dog took me there. But I was able to stand up on it. From there, I could reach over to the dam wall. I pulled myself out by grabbing on to some wooden steps.'

Somehow Ziggy must have communicated to Stella with his strange, high-pitched howl and Stella wasted no time arriving at the scene. 'Ziggy is a very light dog. So I think he knew he couldn't do anything for me himself. But then, I had never seen Stella in the water before. Rottweilers are not water dogs. It makes what she did that much more heroic.' Both dogs showed great qualities. Ziggy's instincts as a collie would normally be to protect his flock from trouble, but being too small to help he used his intelligence to seek help elsewhere and Stella's quick appreciation of the danger and decisive action shows the cleverness and bravery of rottweilers.

RIKI

Everyone knows that cats hate getting wet, so it is no surprise that there are no cases of them diving in to save their owners from treacherous waters. Nevertheless, cats have indirectly saved human lives from drowning.

Lola Del-Costa and her husband, Ernesto, were flying in his private plane from their home in Italy to Spain for a holiday when the engine cut out and they were forced to ditch in the sea. They got clear of the wreckage and into the water, with Ernesto losing blood from a bad cut. Before the crash, he had managed to send an SOS that was picked up by a number of vessels. They searched the area, but three hours later it grew dark and the search party gave up any hope of finding them alive.

On board one of the search vessels, the Italian cargo ship *Lattuga*, was Riki the ship's cat. In the thick of the darkness he suddenly darted to the port side, where he began miaowing loudly and running excitedly backwards and forwards. Captain Diego Suni ordered spot-lights off the prow and a few minutes later they picked out Lola in the water. A deckhand dived in and lifted her aboard alive, although sadly her husband Ernesto was never found. Riki's alertness is owed to the powerful night vision all cats possess. The reflective layer at the back of their eyes helps them catch much more light than human eyes, which is after all why we call the reflective studs in road markings 'cat's eyes'.

PRISCILLA

It is not just dogs and cats that have helped save people from water accidents. Priscilla, a pet pig, won the Stillman Award in 1984 for saving a boy from drowning. Priscilla's owner, Ada Davis, and friends had taken the three-month-old pet pig to Lake Somerville in Texas, where Priscilla went for a swim wearing her harness and leash. A young boy, Anthony Burk, was trying to swim when he got into difficulties, panicked and disappeared underwater. Anthony's mother Clare was too far away to help and it was Priscilla who swam over quickly and reached him just in time. Anthony was exhausted, but managed to grab hold of her leash. Even though Anthony was four times heavier than Priscilla and dragged her under with his weight, she pulled the boy in tow back to shore. It was an astonishing display of intelligence and strength, and Priscilla became a celebrity in Houston.

Pigs are in fact highly intelligent and sociable creatures and, if taken as piglets, make great pets – almost dog-like in their affection and loyalty. They get these great characteristics from the wild boars they descend from. Female boars roam in herds with their piglets, helping each other whenever danger threatens, and this is perhaps why Priscilla took such a keen interest in the boy's troubles.

* * *

DOGGED DEFENCE

Dogs have shown extraordinary bravery in rescuing their owners from much larger animals, by creating diversions at great risk to their own lives. These incidents have often happened when farm animals turn unexpectedly violent.

BAILEY

Farmer Chester Jenkins from Missouri was out in a field feeding his cows and bull when, as he turned his back to open a gate, the bull charged, knocking him down and trampling him into the mud. 'Before I could get up, it tossed me ten yards into a watering trough. When I tried to get out he charged again,' he said. He thought he was going to die when his two-year-old Labrador-retriever called Bailey rushed up. 'Snarling, teeth bared, he shot like a cannonball straight at the bull and sank his fangs into its nose.'

The bull tossed his head with rage and pain, waving Bailey around with it, but the dog refused to let go, giving time for Chester to escape. Only when his master was safe did Bailey run, too. Chester was rushed to hospital with six broken ribs, a punctured lung and a broken shoulderblade, but he recovered. What makes Bailey's heroics especially remarkable is that Labradors and retrievers are usually not very intelligent when faced with unfamiliar situations.

KAMIKAZE COWS

Dogs have also behaved against their basic instincts to save people from manic cows. Barbara Shenton had just helped a heifer calve on her farm near Medicine Hat in Alberta, Canada in March 1996, when the heifer got up, turned round and pinned Barbara in the stall. 'This cow had no intention of getting off my rib cage. As she bellowed and butted my body around, I believed my life over,' Barbara said. She could only scream and, despite training her six-month-old rottweiler puppy to stay away from the cows' pens, he rushed up growling and snapping to get the cow's attention away from Barbara and letting her escape. Luckily, she suffered no broken bones, but undoubtedly owed her life to the dog.

Similarly, Corinne Douglas was saved by her hound Sparky after she was trampled by a herd of angry cattle whilst walking in a field in Wales. Sparky ran behind the cows and barked madly to create a diversion long enough for Corinne to drag herself clear. And in New Zealand, when Lynne Hawkins was attacked by a steer on her farm in Westland, her pet beagle, Tipple, repeatedly bit the steer's back legs until Lynne could run for safety.

In all these cases, the dogs were not only courageous but also employed great cunning to take the attacking animals' attention away from their owner.

CARLETTA

Dogs are not the only heroic pets to save their owners from savage beasts. Carletta, a pet cow, saved her owner from a wild boar in rural Italy in June 1986. Her owner, Bruno Cipriano, was cutting wood on his small hill farm when a huge boar attacked, knocking him to the ground and goring him with its tusks. Suddenly there was a loud moo and Carletta charged at the wild animal, butting it with her horns and chasing it away. Bruno's wife Rosa came out of their house to see what the fuss was about and discovered her bleeding husband on the ground with the cow standing guard over him. Clearly Carletta had formed such a close bond with Bruno after being with him on the farm for ten years, that she protected him like one of her own herd. Or as Bruno himself put it, 'We have a great affection for each other.'

SHEBA

Other pets have saved humans from much more exotic species of fauna. Pieter Erasmus from South Africa was out with a hunting party trying to track down a badly wounded lion that was attacking people at the Olifants River Game Reserve. Suddenly Sheba, his six-year-old bitch, sensed danger in some bushes. She rushed in and found the lion, but was badly mauled by it. Thanks to her alertness and bravery the lion was shot and the search party saved from possible ambush by the beast. Sheba was rushed by plane to a vet's clinic for treatment to her extensive injuries to neck and hind legs. She was later awarded the Animal of the Year Award by the South African Society for the Prevention of Cruelty to Animals.

FLASH

Cats are not well known for physically protecting their owners, but the American magazine *Cat Fancy* published a letter from Kelli Kinsman of Dracut, Massachusetts, about her half-Siamese which saved her from attack by a huge dog. Kelli was five months pregnant and returning to her home through her backyard, when the dog suddenly appeared, attacking her and knocking her down. 'My cat, Flash, flew out the door, wrapped himself around the dog's throat and scratched at his eyes,' Kelli reported. The counter-attack worked and the dog ran away yelping, while eight pounds eight ounces Flash stood hissing at its rapidly retreating back. Perhaps Flash recognised how vulnerable his mistress was in her pregnancy, although his gallant rescue was untypical of cats, which tend to be less inclined than dogs are to help their owners.

Some animals have organised posses to rescue humans under attack and, although the following story is not strictly about pets rescuing people, it reveals the basic instincts of some wild animals to save human life.

Martin Richardson was swimming with dolphins in the Red Sea off Egypt's Sinai peninsula in the summer of 1996 when a shark attacked. It charged through the water, ripped into his chest, then tore into his left shoulder and was passing round for another attack when something extraordinary happened. The dolphins encircled

Martin, flapping their fins and tails to scare away the shark, a defensive behaviour common for mother dolphins trying to protect their calves from predators. They continued their defence until he was pulled aboard a boat to safety. He was then rushed to hospital and received more than two hundred stitches, but he was saved from certain death by the dolphins.

* * *

CANINE-NINE-NINE

In some cases a pet's only way of saving their owner in distress is to run for help. The trouble for an animal is where do they run to and how do they get their message across? What's more, the natural instinct for dogs is to stay with their owner and stand guard over them if they're injured.

TOBY

Toby the terrier belongs to a home for the elderly in Farnham, Surrey and takes a keen interest in the welfare of the residents living there. One day a resident fell unconscious inside her room, but no one heard her apart from Toby, so he sat barking outside her door until the woman was rescued. On another occasion, one of the elderly women was walking along a nearby river when she fell and badly injured herself. Although she could not be seen from the building, Toby somehow realised she was in trouble and started barking and running wildly around the gardens, trying to raise the alarm. One of the care assistants followed him out to the banks of the river where the woman was lying, and she was rescued. In 1995 Toby was awarded an RSPCA bravery medal.

BOB

Of course, dogs are much more than emergency messengers – their acute sense of hearing can alert them to dangers over remarkable distances. One cold winter's day in 1993, Ian Doust was using his motorbike to patrol his parents' vast remote cattle ranch near Narooma, New South Wales, Australia, when it tipped over and threw him off, breaking his leg. The pain was intense but his greatest fear was being left undiscovered in the open, possibly for days. 'I yelled for help, hoping someone would hear me. I even tried bouncing sunlight off my watch in the direction of the neighbours' place – but they didn't pick it up,' he said. Then just as he was starting to get desperate, Bob, his short-tailed border collie cross, turned up at the scene, apparently having picked up his cries from the farmhouse a mile away.

'He was sniffing around, quite depressed by seeing me immobilised there,' said Ian. 'By some miracle I had a pen and a small notepad in my leather jacket. I scrawled a note giving my location and asking for help, folded it over his collar and ordered him home.'

Despite a dog's natural instinct to stay with his owner, Bob obeyed and ran back to Ian's mother, Kath, at the farmhouse. She had no idea why Bob appeared so agitated but as usual she began feeling around his collar for fleas, discovered the note, and rushed to the rescue. Ian was kept in hospital for several days with a severely fractured leg. Bob's great perception and intelligence to run back for help probably saved his master's life.

SEAGULL SAVIOURS

In his book *Psychic Animals* (1987), Dennis Bardens describes how eighty-two-year-old Rachel Flynn of Cape Cod, New England was walking on her own by the coast when she fell over a thirty-foot cliff on to a beach below and was badly hurt. Seagulls hovered over her but amongst them was one that Rachel and her sister fed regularly at their house, and which they called Nancy. The bird flew off to Rachel's sister, June, at home two miles away and continually tapped the window with its beak until June eventually followed the bird to her fallen sister. 'It was simply incredible,' she told reporters, 'the way she came to the window and caused all that racket.' How a bird can show such great intelligence in raising help is a mystery.

2

Pets Against Crimes

One of the ancient duties of dogs was guarding property and persons. A Roman mosaic preserved at Pompeii shows a dog on a lead with the caption Cave Canem, *'Beware of the Dog'. But some dogs have gone much further than simply guarding their owners – they have used their ingenuity and bravery to foil all sorts of fiendish crimes. And not just dogs, because cats have also played heroic roles in policing their neighbourhoods.*

* * *

BARKING BURGLAR ALARMS

SUKI

One dark evening in April 1996, David Brown was at home in South Shields in northern England when his Persian cat, Suki, suddenly woke and leaped up, arched her back and began spitting and scratching at the door. Although the cat had a rather grumpy personality, this kind of behaviour was completely out of character, so David decided to investigate what was troubling her. 'When I let her out she raced into the back garden and I noticed someone was there,' he explained. As he went over to investigate, a man ran off – he had disturbed a burglar trying to break into the next door neighbours' house and the villain was forced to flee empty handed. The next day Suki behaved strangely again, and this time when David investigated he caught the burglar redhanded breaking in next door. Although the villain escaped, the house was never burgled again and Suki proved that cats can be good burglar alarms thanks to their acute sense of hearing.

JESS

One night in April 1996, David Muirhead and his family were asleep in their isolated farmhouse at Dumbarton in Scotland, when a thief broke into the barn next door and stole his motorbike. David heard nothing, but his faithful border collie Jess certainly did, and launched an epic pursuit over forty miles through the dark until the bike ran out of fuel and the thief abandoned it on a hillside. 'We couldn't believe it when the police called and told us they had found Jess on top of the bike,' said David. Jess, however, suffered bleeding paws and exhaustion, but once she had recovered insisted on sleeping in the barn with the motorbike rather than staying in the farmhouse. Maybe she saw the motorbike as one of her flock in need of rounding up!

* * *

FOILED ROBBERIES

BUSTER

One winter's afternoon in November 1989, a pensioner and his dog were both hailed as heroes after putting two armed robbers to flight. A security van was delivering money to a Post Office in a suburb of Birmingham, when the pair of masked criminals ambushed the security guards with a shotgun and pistol. Just then, Christopher Wyton and his Staffordshire bull terrier, Buster, accidentally walked on to the scene. 'One of the robbers, who looked like a giant, told

Staffordshire terrier Buster helped thwart an armed robbery by fearlessly attacking two desperate criminals who fled empty-handed and well bitten.
(Birmingham Post and Mail)

me to push off,' described sixty-seven-year-old Mr Wyton, who stands only five feet tall. He set Buster on to one of the robbers, who sunk his teeth into the man's arm, while Mr Wyton beat the other armed man with his walking stick until the robber suddenly fired his sawn-off shotgun into the pavement. Both Mr Wyton and Buster backed off, but the villains fled empty-handed down the street, jumped into a car and escaped. Police were astonished at the heroism of both pensioner and dog.

*　　*　　*

ANIMALS AGAINST ABDUCTION

Most dogs are naturally protective of their owners, so if they see the human attacked they often instinctively jump to the rescue, which is probably why there are many cases of dogs defending their owners and especially toddlers from abduction.

PLUTO

One summer's afternoon on 23 August 1991, nineteen-month-old Joseph Walter was playing in his front garden in Wolverhampton when a woman walked in and tried to snatch him. Pluto, the family's pet Alsatian, immediately grabbed on to the toddler's trousers with his powerful jaws and hung on so tenaciously that the woman gave up the tug-of-war with the child and fled.

BEN

Potential abductors don't always get off so lightly. In November 1995, Labrador-cross Ben was playing in a park with his owner, Sharon Fossey, and her four-month-old baby, Jordan. Suddenly Ben stopped, snarled and ran straight past Sharon. 'When I turned round I saw someone pushing the buggy away,' explained Sharon. Ben sank his teeth into the abductor's leg but the abductor broke free and ran off limping, leaving baby Jordan behind, safe in her buggy.

JORDY

Staff nurse Catherine Hughes was pounced on by two men when she became lost and tried to reverse her car out from a cul-de-sac in Liverpool on 6 May 1996. But her two-year-old retriever, Jordy, was in the car and leaped up, chasing the men away. 'He must have known something was wrong and suddenly appeared barking and snarling,' explained Catherine. 'One of the men twisted my arm behind my back and forced me to stand between him and the dog. But Jordy took no notice and went for him. He chased after him, then bit him.'

LUCKY

In March 1989, two months after rescuing an abandoned puppy she called Lucky, Mandy Ireland stopped her car with the dog on board when she saw a man lying apparently injured in a quiet layby at Uppingham, Leicestershire. She thought he was a hit-and-run victim and dashed out to help. But the man leaped up, grabbed her and demanded money. When she told him she was broke, he replied: 'Right, I'm taking you for a ride,' Mandy later recalled. The abductor didn't get a chance. Lucky pounced out of the car in a flash, sprinted towards the man baring his fangs and the man ran off. Mandy said: 'Normally he is so timid because he was so obviously ill-treated as a puppy, but he was as brave as a lion.'

MAX

The value of a dog in saving children from abduction was well demonstrated one August evening in 1988. Eleven-year-old Vicky Clark was walking her terrier dog Max through her village, Kippax, near Leeds in Yorkshire. They had turned off the high street into a quiet road near the school when Vicky became aware of a car slowly drawing up. The driver enquired about directions and then asked her if she would like to get in the back of the car. Her suspicions turned to alarm when a man wearing a balaclava mask jumped out of the back of the car and told her to get in. She backed away but the man grabbed her, putting his hand over her mouth. Max immediately attacked. Although he had never bitten anyone before in his life, he sank his teeth deep into the man's hand and, while he was screaming in agony, Vicky escaped. The attacker and his accomplice then made off in their car. The police were deeply moved by the bravery of Max, and Vicky's stepfather said, 'Max has been no sort of guard dog and normally doesn't even bark if someone comes to the door. But he must have realised what was happening and now he's very much on guard if a stranger approaches the house.' It was indeed an heroic act for such a small dog, bred for chasing mice and rats, to attack a grown man.

*   *   *

PET PROTECTION

Dogs are not the only animals used for protecting life and property. Professional burglar Jonathan Lomas was breaking into a house in Houston, Texas one winter's night in 1993, when he was rudely interrupted by a 200lb pig charging at him. He was knocked to the ground and pinned there by the hog until the police arrived and arrested him. Owner Rick Charles said he bought the pig for meat but couldn't bring himself to kill her after her heroic feat. Animal behaviourists say that pet pigs have many dog-like qualities in their affection and loyalty to their owners, but they may also attack outsiders if they feel threatened, which is why this particular pig proved worth its bacon.

HEIDI

In 1992, Heidi, a German shepherd/Doberman mix from Blissfield, Michigan actually prevented an accident. As fifteen-month-old toddler Kristiana Hosler was playing in the front yard of their home, she wandered out into the street and was about to step into the path of an oncoming car when Heidi leaped out, grabbed her by the back of her trousers and pulled her back. Even more remarkable is that Heidi had only been adopted by the Hoslers just three days beforehand.

German shepherd dogs and Dobermans are two of the most intelligent breeds of dogs and Heidi showed great foresight in realising the danger and reacting in a split-second.

JAMBO

Other creatures have undeserved reputations for being aggressive. When a five-year-old boy fell twenty feet into a gorilla enclosure in Jersey Zoo in September 1986, he was rescued by a male gorilla, Jambo. The twenty-five-year-old, eighteen-stone primate kept the other gorillas at bay as young Levan Merriott lay unconscious in the enclosure. When Levan began whimpering, Jambo gently stroked the boy's face until human rescuers arrived. Levan later recovered in hospital from head and arm injuries and Jambo's act of kindness was commemorated with a life-sized bronze sculpture of himself. However, we have tended to misunderstand gorillas, who are generally peaceful creatures rarely given to violence unless provoked.

✻ ✻ ✻

DRUG SNIFFERS

LUISE

One of the German police's top drug sniffers scored a remarkable run of drug seizures and became a national celebrity, yet she was dogged by controversy. She was a pig called Luise. As a piglet, Luise caught the eye of police dog handler Werner Franke, who saw that she was sociable, curious, and like most pigs had a superb sense of smell – all ideal qualities for a top drugs sniffer. She was very easy to train to detect both drugs and explosives, even when buried seventy centimetres underground, and often beat the force's top sniffer dogs. She also got on so well with the police force's dogs she even shared a kennel with a rottweiler.

It wasn't an entirely happy story, though. Luise soon caught the attention of the German media, and state officials started worrying that she was giving the police a bad image, so they suspended her from work. So great was the public outcry when she departed that the authorities reprieved her, although demands that all police dogs be replaced by pigs were rejected outright. Such was her fame that Luise went on to hog the limelight, making a goodwill tour of Berlin where she appeared on stage during a special Christmas show, and was declared an official civil servant in 1985. She eventually retired in February 1987 to raise a family. Pigs make excellent sniffers because they have a powerful sense of smell inherited from their wild boar ancestors who foraged for food by rooting around on forest floors. They are intelligent enough to be trained and, despite their dirty reputation, pigs are naturally clean creatures which use special dunging areas if given the opportunity.

WINSTON

As we have witnessed, dogs have a highly developed sense of smell and intelligent breeds like Alsatians make some of the best drug sniffers. In fact, some sniffer dogs have become so successful they have been targeted by criminals. Police dog Winston became the top drugs sniffer in the US, catching a total of £50 million in hauls of cocaine. He could even sniff out crack cocaine in rooms scattered with mothballs or covered in coffee to disguise the smell. Then in March 1989, he intercepted a £5 million shipment of cocaine from New York, and this enormous seizure enraged Mafia drug bosses so much they put a £1 million contract on Winston's life. As Don Lambert, the local sheriff in Orange County, California revealed: 'He is on the hit list of the biggest drug dealers in the US. Even the Medellin drug barons from Columbia want him dead.' From then on Winston was kept under close guard but successfully carried on with his duties.

Top police dog Jake 'One' became so successful at sniffing out drugs that he was abducted by drug barons and narrowly avoided execution. (David Dalton)

JAKE 'ONE'

The Irish police suffered a much worse ordeal with their own top drug-busting dog called Jake. In an illustrious career spanning three years, Jake uncovered more than £9 million of heroin. He became so successful he was kidnapped on the orders of drugs barons, who offered £10,000 for his execution. In 1994 Jake vanished after being snatched from his handler's home and soon afterwards the police learned that he was due to be killed on 31 May. Such was the importance attached to Jake that the police launched a major search and made public appeals on radio and television for information on his whereabouts. It was this publicity that probably helped to save him, because the kidnappers were too afraid to move him out of the area before the execution. At the very last moment, at 2.30 a.m. on 31 May, Jake was discovered barking madly in a shed behind an empty house near Wexford and was rescued, later resuming normal duties with his nose for smuggling.

* * *

SENSATIONAL DISCOVERIES

A dog's natural curiosity and acute sense of smell have led to some sensational discoveries over the years.

JAKE 'TWO'

One December's day in 1985, John Winch was fossil hunting on a beach on the Isle of Wight when Jake, his bull terrier, began busily scrabbling in the sand. When John looked to see what was preoccupying his dog, he was amazed to discover a collosal bone. Jake had unearthed one of the finest ever dinosaur fossils: a 118-million-year-old, four-feet long iguanadon armbone from an animal which would originally have stood twenty-five feet tall. 'When we finally dug it out and laid it on the beach I thought it was something special – even if it did look like a giant dog bone,' John told newspaper reporters. Geologists were especially pleased with the find because complete bones of any dinosaur are quite rare. This specimen was also very well preserved and one of the largest found in Britain.

Bull terrier Jake 'Two' bit off more than he could chew when he dug up one of the world's best-preserved dinosaur bones. (Isle of Wight News Agency)

PICKLES

A mongrel dog called Pickles became a world celebrity in 1966. Out for a summer evening's walk with his owner, Dave Corbett, along a leafy suburban street in Norwood, south London, the one-year-old pup suddenly disappeared into a hedge and refused to budge. Corbett discovered Pickles transfixed by a small package wrapped in newspaper. It was twelve inches high and made of solid gold – Pickles the dog had found the football World Cup, stolen just after the 1966 soccer final. 'I took it back indoors to show my wife. I couldn't believe it for a few minutes, then I got into the car and took it to the police,' said Corbett. The Jules Rimet Trophy had been stolen seven days earlier from an exhibition in London, where the Football Association had reluctantly allowed it to be shown on condition that there would be a twenty-four-hour guard. 'Nothing at all went wrong with our security,' one of the organisers told reporters. 'The cup just got stolen.' The thief then tried to extort money for the safe return of the cup. A nationwide police investigation was launched but the thief was never caught. Pickles was rewarded with a year's supply of dog food by Spillers, awarded a medal by the Canine Defence League, and later starred with June Whitfield in a film called *The Spy With a Cold Nose*.

3

Paws on the Pulse

Pets seem to have an uncanny sense of knowing when their owners are seriously ill, sometimes before any obvious symptoms appear. To recognise what are often subtle differences in human behaviour takes great perception, and probably shows how closely cats and dogs observe and know their owners. But the following stories also demonstrate that pets are ingenious at taking emergency action: fetching help, giving physical support, and even giving first aid. Indeed, animals are so good at helping out in medical crises that they have great promise for being trained for medical life-saving in the future.

* * *

YELP FOR HELP

The following stories are all remarkable because the pets first of all realised that their owners were in dire trouble and then used their ingenuity to fetch help.

JOAD

Joad the collie watched helplessly when his master, Dennis Horrell, fell to the floor of his home in a diabetic coma. The eight-year-old dog could not rouse him and, realising the situation was desperate, went outside into the street in New Marske near Middlesborough and barked for help until neighbours came out to see what the trouble was. Joad led them indoors where Mr Horrell lay unconscious. An ambulance was called and Mr Horrell was taken to hospital, where he made a full recovery.

Stories like Joad's are not unusual. When diabetic Candy Sangster of Sepulvedra, California slipped into a coma her Doberman pinscher also sought help by running next door and barking at the neighbours. Similarly, eight-year-old collie Tripper ran for help when his master, Jim Rigg, fell on a beach during an epileptic fit as the tide was racing in. What is so remarkable about these three dogs is that their natural instinct would be stay with their owner, yet they all had the intelligence to seek help.

GEMMA

Dogs have even sought help by answering the phone in an emergency. Darren Mahon fell unconscious during an epileptic fit at his home in Erdington, Birmingham in January 1996. His mongrel, Gemma, was locked indoors and could do nothing to help. But when the phone rang, Gemma knocked the phone off its hook and barked furiously down the mouthpiece. Realising that something was wrong, the neighbour at the other end of the line rushed round to the house and found Gemma watching over Darren, and called for an ambulance. The dog had probably seen the phone used enough times to realise that it carried messages, but to use that information in a crisis was a stroke of real brilliance.

LYRIC

An eight-year-old Irish setter called Lyric went one better – she actually rang up the emergency services. On 10 March 1996, asthma sufferer Judi Bayly collapsed unconscious in her home in Nashua, New Hampshire and only Lyric was there to help. She knocked the receiver off the hook, hit three pre-programmed buttons for the emergency services and barked furiously until the call was traced.

Judi was found and later recovered. 'I feel like I've got some kind of guardian angel sleeping on my bed with me – even if it's red with a fur coat,' she explained. It was a showpiece of canine intelligence.

* * *

RESCUE MISSIONS

SPARKY

Apart from using their brains and senses, pets have also used their physical strength to make some remarkable rescue missions. Sparky, a loyal and loveable Labrador retriever from Tullahoma, Tennessee was being taken out for an early walk one winter's morning in 1992 when his owner, John Culbertson, collapsed to the ground with a heart attack. Sparky was so desperate to help he dragged his 227lb owner home by turning backwards and pulling him nearly 200 yards back to the front door. He barked madly until John's wife Dorothy found them and rushed her husband to hospital, where he was saved. It was an amazing feat of strength by Sparky, and recalls the days a century or so ago when dogs were frequently used for hauling carts of goods through streets.

* * *

RESCUE CUDDLES

HUSH PUPPIES

One of the most common ways pets have saved their owners' lives is by wrapping themselves around them and keeping them warm in freezing conditions. It is probably an instinct inherited from wolf packs huddling together. An amazing example of this occurred when three-year-old Robbie Campbell went missing in woods in Mount

Airy, North Carolina in 1994. He had last been seen wearing only light clothes and playing with his three puppies. Searchers combed the woods all night in the cold and eventually found him with the three puppies wrapped around him – one under his head, the other two spread out on top. 'He looked as though he was snuggled inside a fur blanket,' said his mother Debra. He was rushed to hospital suffering from hypothermia and though doctors found that his body temperature had fallen from 98.4°F to 94°F, unquestionably the puppies had saved his life with their warmth.

WILD DOGS

There are dozens of other stories of pet dogs keeping their owners warm in the bitter cold, and this is so instinctive that even wild dogs have cuddled up to humans, as the following case shows – a story that is strangely reminiscent of the legend of Romulus and Remus. One cold spring morning in March 1996, ten-year-old Josh Carlisle wandered away from his home in Cassville, Missouri into the surrounding woods. But when temperatures fell to 2°F and he failed to return, his mother Jenny raised the alarm and police and locals then spent the next seventy-two hours searching the dense hilly woodland. Hopes of finding Josh alive were fading when one of the search party heard a pair of wild dogs barking at him and saw a body next to them. 'I saw the boy lying down and the big dog next to him was barking,' he described. The dogs had apparently adopted Josh and kept him warm for so long he smelled of them, but apart from slight frostbite he was otherwise unharmed. One theory is that the animals may have appeared in the past at the Carlisles' remote home in search of food and that Josh gave them scraps. When they saw the boy again in the woods they assumed he was friendly and decided to look after him. Animal psychologists say the dogs' behaviour illustrates their social nature and that they would have lain down with Josh when they realised he was in distress.

FLUFFY

Cats, too, seem instinctively to cuddle up to people in need of warmth. Margaret Weir, a nurse at an old peoples' home in Nottingham, was puzzled when her Persian cat, Fluffy, refused to come in after her evening prowl. She went out looking for her and found Fluffy sitting beside a bundle of rags, keeping it company and miaowing to get her attention. 'I thought it was just a pile of rubbish,' she said. 'But when I looked closer I saw a hand. Then I heard a child whimpering.' It was a baby girl, weighing 7lbs 8oz, abandoned in a sack. She later recovered in hospital. Clearly, cats can have just as much compassion as dogs when it comes to sharing cuddles.

SLOWLY CAT

One bitterly cold winter's night, Virgil and Linda McMillan searched in vain for their cat called Slowly Cat, who had gone out in temperatures plunging to $-12°F$. Next day she was still missing, but when Virgil found an old sack at the rear of their home and was about to throw it away, Slowly Cat crawled out of it and then back in again. Virgil wondered what was inside and found himself staring in disbelief at a baby boy in the bottom, with Slowly Cat curled round him, licking his face. He rushed the baby to the local hospital, where he was treated by Dr Alan Randolph for hypothermia. 'He could have died if the cat had not snuggled into the sack with him,' commented Dr Randolph. 'The licking and the animal's body heat helped keep the child alive.'

SAMANTHA

On a crisp, cold winter's day in 1992, the Johnston family of Ontario were celebrating the birth of their new baby. Three-year-old Donald Johnston was at home with his father Darryl in Tiny Township, while his mother was recovering in hospital thirty miles away in Barrie. But Donald wanted to see his mother and, unnoticed by his father, he slipped outside and started walking down the road towards the hospital. He had covered almost a kilometre in freezing cold temperatures and was beginning to suffer from exposure when he was spotted on the road by an Alsatian dog, Samantha, who immediately came up and nuzzled next to him. Donald put his arm round the dog, she licked his face in return and led him into her home well away from the road. Samantha's owner Brian Holmes was amazed to see his dog with a boy who was so cold he couldn't talk. Meanwhile, Donald's father Darryl had been searching frantically for his son and eventually tracked him down to the Holmes' house. Had Samantha the friendly Alsatian not befriended Donald along his epic journey he would undoubtedly have collapsed with hypothermia.

* * *

FURRY FIRST AID

Most of the cases of pet heroism we have looked at so far have to some extent probably involved an animal's instinct. But these next few cases seem to defy instinct. They show that many dogs must be watching their owners so keenly they can read very subtle changes in behaviour. They can not only tell when they are seriously unwell but with their intelligence also administer highly effective first aid without any proper training. These stories may seem unbelievable but they tend to fit a recognisable pattern of behaviour.

BYRON

Arthur Whittled was watching a video in his living room at home in Redditch, Birmingham when he started gasping for breath and then stopped breathing altogether. His daughter who was in the room at the time shouted for help and her mother called an ambulance. When the ambulance crew arrived they were giving Arthur air when suddenly the family dog, Byron, pushed past them and leaped on his chest. To their amazement, Arthur gave a spluttering cough and started to breathe again.

BEN

Maureen Bulmer, from Milton Keynes in Buckinghamshire, suffers from a rare disorder which occasionally creates an air bubble in the back of her throat, suffocating and paralysing her. Normally her husband Terence cures it by knocking the back of her neck to dislodge the air bubble, but one day he had gone out to the shops leaving Maureen alone in the house with their sheepdog, Ben. 'I was doing some cleaning in the bathroom upstairs when I felt ill,' Maureen recalled. 'I immediately panicked. There was no way I could call for help.' She slumped to the floor, fighting for breath. Ben was downstairs and must have heard her fall because he came rushing into the bathroom, barking. 'I stared at him in desperation – if only he could understand and help me,' Maureen said. 'Suddenly he jumped on my back. It was so strange – it was as if he knew exactly what he was doing. He jumped again and broke the air bubble. I could breathe again.' Like many dogs, Ben was probably a keen observer of his owners and perhaps he realised what treatment was needed when Maureen was in trouble.

HOLLY

A West Highland terrier called Holly came to the rescue when her owner fell into a diabetic coma at home in Cambridge on 3 April 1996. Roz Brown felt unwell and started to walk to her sitting room to rest when she collapsed unconscious as her blood sugar level fell dangerously low. Holly immediately ran over to a bag of jelly babies on a table, tipped two of them on the floor by Roz's nose and then nuzzled her mistress's head to rouse her. 'When I came round slightly I saw these two sweets by my face and Holly sitting by the back of my head,' Roz explained. She was just about able to put the sweets in her mouth, which revived her enough to allow her to stagger into the kitchen and eat enough food to bring her sugar level back to normal. 'I often have a jelly baby if I feel unwell and

Holly must have seen me eating them,' explained Roz. But how Holly understood that Roz was ill and that the sweets would save her and then had the intelligence to bring them over to her is extraordinary.

TRIXIE

In all these examples, the dog had probably learned by observation what first aid treatment was needed. But the next story is incredible because the dog concerned had never seen how to resuscitate a human, and had to use its own initiative entirely. In December 1991, seventy-five-year-old Jack Fyfe suffered a paralysing stroke at his home in Eastwood, Sydney. His only companion was his six-year-old kelpie-border collie cross dog, Trixie, who somehow realised he was dehydrating and soaked a towel in her water bowl and brought it to him to suck. Once the water bowl had dried up, Trixie then dropped the towel into the toilet to wet it again, and returned with it to revive Jack. She kept this remarkable lifeline going for nine days until help finally arrived when a neighbour called in and discovered Jack severely distressed but still alive. If it had not been for Trixie's extraordinary life-saving skills he would have died of dehydration.

* * *

DOCTOR DOGS

It may stretch our imagination to its limits, but pets have warned their owners of dangerous illnesses. In fact, medical authorities are recognising the potential for using animals' amazing powers of perception to detect serious human medical conditions before anyone else has noticed. But how do they do it? If it was simply a matter of learning the minute details of their owners' habits this perception might be easy to understand. But pets often pick up signals from people they hardly know, such as newborn babies, or in homes they have newly been adopted in. Either these animals rapidly learn to recognise things out of the ordinary, or they have senses we simply do not appreciate. Whatever the explanation, these next stories all show a remarkably similar pattern of pet behaviour that lends added credibility to their claims.

SAM

Sam the collie is Alan Harberd's medical watchdog at his home in Cambridge. Alan is diabetic and every time his blood sugar level drops dangerously low while he is asleep, five-year-old Sam is ready to warn him any time throughout the night. Once Sam senses the danger, he wakes Alan up and prevents him slipping into a coma. 'He always manages to wake me just before the critical time, when my blood sugar is low but not so low I can't get up and do something about it,' says Alan. 'It is touch and go sometimes, but it is uncanny the way he does it.' Sam apparently never gives a false alarm, but how he picks up the danger signs isn't certain: it could be that he detects a telltale smell on Alan's breath or from his sweat, which increases as his blood sugar level drops.

BOO

One feat of medical diagnosis by a dog was so extraordinary it was written up in a medical journal. Bonita Whitfield felt in perfectly good health, but her dog Boo kept on sniffing one of her legs so much that eventually Bonita noticed that Boo was particularly attracted to a mole. She went to her doctor who referred her to King's College Hospital London, where dermatologist Dr Hywel Williams discovered that the mole was cancerous and successfully removed it. How could Boo have known something was wrong and tried to alert her owner? Dr Williams believes that she scented the cancer at a very early stage and he and his colleague Dr Andrew Pembroke proposed, in a letter to *The Lancet* in April 1989, that malignant tumours might give off unique odours that dogs can pick up, and that they should seriously be considered for use in detecting

Dog diagnosis – Bonita Whitfield's dog Boo alerted her to a cancerous mole on her leg by constantly sniffing and biting the tumour, possibly detecting it by smell. (Eddie Mulholland)

the early signs of skin cancer. Boo herself was rewarded with the PRO Dogs gold medal in 1989.

MIDNIGHT

Cats can also make life-saving diagnoses and summon help, as this story from *Cat Fancy* magazine shows. Bernita Rogers of Kansas City, Missouri was in her living room one night after putting her six-week-old baby Stacey to bed. The baby had been suffering from a breathing infection but that night went to sleep easily in her cot. Suddenly the family cat, Midnight, grew very agitated. 'He was jumping in my lap, batting at my leg and generally making a noise,' said Bernita. 'This was unusual behaviour for our normally quiet, docile cat.'

After telling him off several times, Midnight sulked off. Then Bernita heard the cat crying through the baby's intercom monitor from the nursery, and she ran upstairs to investigate.

'When I arrived, the scene was eerie. Midnight was perched on the dresser by the monitor looking into the cot and literally crying, for lack of a better description. Stacey was in marked respiratory distress – she was blue and gasping for breath.' Bernita rushed the baby to hospital in Kansas City where she was placed on a respirator, and later recovered. How Midnight knew there was something drastically wrong with the baby shows how alert he must have been to her, even though she was only a few weeks old. But to then draw attention to the crisis was a highly intelligent act, and won Midnight the *Cat Fancy* magazine's grand prize of 1986.

PAPILLON

Some pets seem to have an affinity for babies. In June 1993, five-week-old baby Rachel Dorfman-Wynne was put to bed in her nursery as normal and her mother, Mindi, went for a shower in the bathroom. Five minutes later her collie, Papillon, burst in barking. 'I yelled, but he wouldn't shut up,' says Mindi. Papillon ran off and Mindi followed him to the nursery where he jumped up against the cradle, barking furiously. Then she noticed that the baby's lips were blue and she had stopped breathing. Mindi frantically gave mouth-to-mouth resuscitation until an ambulance arrived, but fortunately Rachel had recovered by then. Tests showed that the baby had suffered reflux, a potentially fatal condition in which an infant's airway becomes blocked. Perhaps Papillon had grown so familiar with the baby's breathing patterns that he could pick up the danger signs and then knew when help was needed. It was an extraordinary act of intelligence and earned him a hero's medal from the Humane Society of the United States.

TINA

Tina, a one-year-old mixed breed dog, was found abandoned and adopted by the Martyniak family from Lakeville, Massachusetts. Then early one evening just two weeks later in March 1992 she saved the life of her new owner when she raced into the living room, where Mr Martyniak lay apparently fast asleep. Because of Tina's relentless furore, Nora Anna Martyniak rushed in from the kitchen and discovered that her husband had stopped breathing. 'I found Tina on top of my husband's chest with her mouth right next to his – almost as if she was trying to give him her breath.' Nora Ann called for an ambulance and Tina continued to bark and tug on Mr Martyniak's shirt until the paramedics arrived, just in time to revive him. Mr Martyniak had no previous medical problems and had suffered an unexplained convulsion. 'At first glance he actually looked asleep,' said Nora Ann. 'If it weren't for Tina's actions I might never have taken a closer look.' She was mystified by the dog's actions, but is certain her husband would not be alive today had it not been for her. It is remarkable how Tina knew something was wrong, especially as she was in another room at the time. The only rational explanation is that she could hear Mr Martyniak's breathing stop, thanks to a dog's naturally good hearing, and knew that was a dangerous sign. Having only lived in her new owners' house for two weeks, Tina must have learned their behaviours rapidly. Maybe it was a sign of how close she felt to them for adopting her.

RUPERT

As the canine world showed off its best specimens at Crufts dog show on 17 March 1996, one woman's life was saved by her dog. Tony Brown-Griffin is an epileptic and the owner of Rupert, a three-year-old collie who can predict the onset of a fit up to forty minutes beforehand and warn her with a characteristic bark.

As she was walking through the dog show, Rupert jumped in front of her, barked, and Tony sought out a safe place and prepared for a fit. 'Without Rupert, I would not have the time to prepare and would not know that a fit was approaching until it was too late,' said Tony. 'The medical experts hate attributing it to a "sixth sense", but Rupert hasn't failed me yet. I've learned to distinguish between his barking to indicate an epileptic fit and what is simply playful. He has undoubtedly saved my life on numerous occasions.'

BRUNO

Other dogs have also shown similar powers of predicting epileptic fits. Bruno is a Jack Russell who instinctively knows when his master, John Stoddart, is about to have a fit. Bruno drops on his stomach, crawls towards his master and makes a fuss of him. Bruno has even been taught to press a button to open a security lock on the front door of their house in Newton Aycliffe, County Durham so that medical help can get in if needed.

Experts are now trying to find out how dogs predict these fits, and research by the British Epilepsy Association has identified a unique smell given off by sufferers during an epileptic attack. It is thought that this odour could be the signal which alerts the dog to an imminent seizure. Alternatively, the animals may detect a change in electrical impulses from the brain, or maybe they can spot small but significant changes in an owner's behaviour. Whatever the explanation, dogs are now being trained by Support Dogs, a Sheffield-based charity, to accompany epileptics and warn them of fits and then fetch help.

Bruno instinctively knows his master, John Stoddart, is about to have an epileptic fit and warns him. Dogs are now being trained to help other sufferers. (David Paton)

4

Pet Premonitions

Some people claim that their pets have premonitions or 'psychic' powers – that they can read their owners' minds, forecast their behaviour or predict disasters. This chapter reports events which are by far the most incredible and difficult to explain by conventional science. It is possible that all the examples are simply bizarre coincidences, and the pets reacted by accident just as an event elsewhere took place. Yet there are so many similar stories coincidence is stretched too far. In fact, we may have to revise our notions about animal awareness and realise that they are much more in tune with the world than is usually appreciated. Quite apart from the academic interest, if we could tap into these powers it might be possible to avert all sorts of disasters, some of them on a huge scale.

* * *

PAWS FOR THOUGHT

Many people say that their cats and dogs have 'psychic' powers and know, for example, when they are about to return home and stand ready at a door or window long before their arrival. In a recent survey in Greater Manchester, forty-six per cent of dog owners and fourteen per cent of cat owners claimed to have noticed the trait. At first it seems a baffling phenomenon. What we often don't realise is that cats and dogs often keep a very close watch on us and can remember our patterns of behaviour in minute detail. They also have a great sense of timekeeping, so it's surprisingly easy for them to learn and then anticipate our routines. Alternatively, they might notice tiny cues from the people around them, like someone checking their watch when a person is due to arrive.

But if the owner doesn't keep to a routine and the people at home don't know what is going to happen, and the animal still anticipates its owner's return, then we have something much more remarkable. The only way to investigate these psychic claims properly is to test them scientifically over and over again until the results can be analysed to see whether these things happen by chance or by design.

JAYTEE

Pam Smart of Ramsbottom, Lancashire claims that her seven-year-old terrier mongrel dog, Jaytee, possesses a mysterious power. Her parents first noticed something unusual when they looked after Jaytee while Pam was at work. Long before she came home from work the dog went to wait by the window, but Pam put this down to a regular schedule which Jaytee had learnt. However, when Pam quit her job as a school secretary in 1993 and started returning at irregular times, Jaytee would still walk over to the window when she was about to set off from her distant location. Pam's mother made a record of when the dog reacted and then compared the times to when Pam had left to return home, and, give or take a few minutes, they generally matched. Jaytee seemed to know the moment Pam prepared to leave for home.

Pam tried to look at it from a sceptic's point of view. 'I thought it might be the sound of the car, so I went in taxis or other people's cars. I even cycled and went on foot to rule that one out,' she explained. She also ruled out any powerful sense of hearing because several times Jaytee has known when she was leaving Blackpool

Are pets psychic? Pam Smart's faithful dog Jaytee knows when Pam is coming home long before her arrival, no matter what the time of day or how she travels. (Gary Taylor)

forty-five miles away and it's simply impossible that any dog could hear that far!

It was possible, however, that the dog might be picking up subtle cues from her parents, so Pam didn't tell them when she was returning home. But the results over three weeks of testing were still the same. Some people might say that the dog is telepathic and picks up Pam's thoughts, but she denies this: 'It's nothing I feel – when I get in the car to come home I am not particularly thinking about Jaytee.'

Biologist Dr Rupert Sheldrake in London has long had an interest in the powers of prediction of animals. He has now carried out 156 tests on Jaytee and found that he successfully anticipated Pam's return home 81 per cent of the time, no matter how long Pam had been away, or how long she had to travel home. The 19 per cent of the time the dog got it wrong were either when he was distracted by visitors such as the postman, or by a neighbourhood bitch on heat!

To see if noise could distract Jaytee, twenty-three experiments were made involving loud banging outside the house as a car was worked on in the street. Although Jaytee went to the window to investigate the commotion outside – which counted as a failure in the experiments – he still successfully predicted Pam's return home 68 per cent of the time.

During these tests, Dr Sheldrake also made sure that Pam couldn't inadvertently let Jaytee know her plans in advance by sending Pam randomly selected times to return home at a few moments' notice using a radio bleeper.

He also complemented these tests by using video cameras to record four-hour periods of Jaytee's behaviour to see when he gazed out of the window and whether this matched the time Pam set off. In two hundred hours of video recording, Jaytee showed a consistently high success rate. Even when Dr Richard Wiseman – a highly sceptic psychologist from Hertfordshire University – repeated the same tests himself, Jaytee scored two out of three successful predictions. This was essentially the same pass rate as Sheldrake's results. Wiseman, however, considered this proof of the dog's failure, which seems unduly harsh.

Another of Dr Sheldrake's test owners is Jan Fennel who believes her seven dogs know when she is *thinking* about taking them for a walk which they anticipate by becoming noisy, boisterous and making for the door. Even though the dogs have no set time for their outings and even though she can be in another part of the house where they can't see her, they still grow excited when she starts thinking about walking them. To test whether they really can read her mind, Jan locked her dogs in the conservatory for a few hours each day with a video camera recording their every movement, while she was in another part of the house doing things ranging from housework to watching television. Then, completely at random, she would spend ten minutes thinking of walking the dogs. Early results from the video seem to show that, at the moment Jan has these thoughts, the dogs jump towards the door and make a noise, having spent most of their time beforehand being fairly inactive. A lot more tests are needed before these results prove significant but early indications are intriguing.

Pam Smart's and Jan Fennel's experiences with their dogs are far from unique. Dr Sheldrake has collected about two thousand similar cases of pets predicting their owners' return from Britain, France, Austria and the USA, and they tend to have an uncannily similar pattern.

TELEPATHY IN GEORGIA

Mrs Louise Gavit of Morrow, Georgia claims that her dog always knows when she wants to return home even though she has no routine or schedule. The dog wakes up, moves to the door, lies there and waits. Louise is convinced it's her thoughts he reacts to: 'He does not respond at all to my leaving one place and moving to another,' she claims. 'His response seems to be apparent at the time I form the thought to return home, and take the action to walk toward my car to come home.' She rules out the dog responding to the sound of her approaching car because she travels in a variety of cars, a truck, driven by herself or other people, and sometimes she walks.

CAYCE

Similarly, Mrs Jan Woody of Dallas, Texas says her dog Cayce also knew when either her husband or herself were leaving work to come home. 'She would stop what she was doing, whether in the yard or in the house, and go sit by the front door at the exact minute my husband or myself left whatever activity we were attending.' There seemed no routine Cayce could learn or cues from her family she could pick up on since none of them knew when the other was coming home. Yet when the couple compared notes afterwards they found Cayce had gone to sit by the door the minute the other partner had left work.

TELEPATHY IN CATS

Although most examples of pets predicting their owners' return tend to feature dogs, there are cases of cats with similar powers. Following an article about animal premonitions in the *Sunday Telegraph* in 1995, several people wrote in with similar stories of cat premonitions. Peggy Matty of Rugeley, Staffordshire had a ginger cat, Bill, who was devoted to her mother and always seemed to know when she was about to visit long before she arrived. 'There, sitting in the drive, would be this little ginger sentinel,' said Mrs Matty. When her mother died, her stepfather continued to visit and drive exactly the same car, but Bill never went out to greet him or the car again. How did he know not to wait any more after his friend had died? It is very difficult to explain.

SIAMESE CATS

Similarly, Mrs Judith Preston-Jones of Paddock Wood, Kent had two Siamese cats which had uncanny powers of perception. Her husband Geoffrey always knew when she was coming home. 'He says that the cats are complete zombies when I am out but come to life shortly before I arrive. He reckons they know when I am about three miles away,' explains Mrs Preston-Jones.

CARLO

Perhaps some stories of psychic pets can be explained if the owners are giving out inadvertent signals. But the case of Marian Rowe was baffling because her cat, Carlo, always seemed to know just in advance when she was phoning home. 'When the phone rang and it was Marian, Carlo would bound up the stairs before I had picked up the receiver,' said her mother Veronica Rowe. 'He never did it at any other time.'

ROSE

Of course, it is possible that sometimes pets can hear things their owners can not. Mrs Phyllis Teage of Dartmouth recounted how her guinea-pig, Rose, would suddenly sit upright on her lap whenever her husband was about to come in. 'She was amazing because I could never hear anything.'

Dr Sheldrake also has cases of parrots and mynah birds, which call out the name of their owner before they return. It is extremely difficult to explain these phenomena, yet despite the vast anecdotal evidence and his preliminary tests, he's run into a brick wall with the orthodox scientific community which refuses to take the subject seriously. As a result, and apart from a small grant from an American foundation, Sheldrake can't get research funds. It's unlikely that conventional scientists will believe this phenomenon exists until the experiments are repeated in a laboratory.

* * *

DEATH AND THE PARANORMAL PET

There have long been stories of pets who have known their owners had died somewhere far away. When the famous Egyptologist Lord Carnarvon discovered the tomb of Tut-ankhamun it's said that the mummy put a curse on him, and two months later on 6 April 1923, he died suddenly and mysteriously in Cairo. According to relatives at home, at exactly the time he died in Egypt his dog in England started howling, although no one at the time knew that his master had passed away.

ARIZONA

This story may have become embellished with time, but similar cases have happened much more recently. Richard H. Lee of Prescott, Arizona was suddenly killed in a car accident far from his home shortly before midnight in 1965. His wife was at home and noticed that at around midnight – long before she received the tragic news – their devoted black tomcat frantically raced backwards and forwards on the front lawn. The cat refused to enter the house or allow her to touch him. 'When I took out some food, he climbed the stone wall at the back of the house in a perfect panic,' she recalled. The cat did not return home, but remained wandering around the neighbourhood for months afterwards. Had the cat received a psychic message that his master had been killed, and then become so unnerved that he couldn't face living at home again? We simply don't know.

WESSEX

Dogs may also have the power of foretelling death much closer to hand. The novelist Thomas Hardy had a wire-haired terrier called Wessex, who was very fond of Hardy's friend William Watkins. But when Watkins visited the Hardy home one spring evening, Wessex started whining at him in the study and several times during the evening tugged Watkins's sleeve with his paw, crying with distress. Both Hardy and his friend were baffled by the dog's behaviour, and when Watkins left the house he was in good spirits and appeared fine. But early next morning Watkins's son called to say his father had died suddenly an hour or so after leaving the Hardys' house. It seemed that Wessex was trying to warn him, but how? With a keen sense of sight and smell, terriers were originally bred for hunting vermin, and it may be that the dog detected something in Watkins's behaviour or smell that alarmed him.

HEIDI

Something similar happened much more recently during the winter of 1974. Heidi was a dachshund-terrier cross belonging to a retired Bank of England official, Frank Ashworth. His mother adored the dog, and when she was taken seriously ill Frank went over to stay with her and took Heidi as well. But the dog grew increasingly restless in his mother's house, jumping off chairs, on to his lap and into her basket. This continued until 11 a.m. the next day, when suddenly she ran into his mother's room, jumped on to her bed and licked her hands and face, as though it were a last kiss. Within an hour his mother died and shortly afterwards Heidi settled down normally.

How pets can sense imminent death may have something to do with the way they can pick up changes in human bodies that we are unaware of (as mentioned in 'Doctor Dogs', pp. 42–8). It could be that they smell a change in body odours, or see changes in human behaviour we simply don't appreciate. There's even a thought that they can pick up the weak electrical field around a human, generated by the electricity in the body's nerves and muscles. But this is all speculation.

*   *   *

TAILS OF THE UNEXPECTED

Premonitions by pets can also be large-scale and involve major disasters. During the Second World War Blitz in Britain, many people claimed that their cats could predict air raids, becoming agitated and noisy well before any warning was sounded, and seagulls would fly away from coastal areas well before the bomber planes arrived.

FAITH

Probably the most famous case of a pet premonition was a tabby and white cat called Faith who lived on the top floor of the church house by St Augustine's Church in the City of London. She was normally a calm creature, but a change suddenly came over her on 6 September 1940. She frantically searched out various corners in the building, until eventually she took herself and her kitten down three floors and hid in a recess in a wall where piles of music sheets were stored. The rector, the Rev. H. Ross, repeatedly tried taking the kitten back upstairs, but Faith always returned the kitten to the recess.

Three nights later the church was heavily bombed, the roofs and masonry collapsed and the whole church set ablaze. Next morning Rev. Ross clambered over the smouldering wreckage and was amazed to find Faith and her kitten alive and unhurt in the recess, sheltered by debris which had fallen on top. News of the amazing escape quickly spread and she soon became a national heroine, and was awarded a silver medal by the People's Dispensary for Sick Animals. How Faith anticipated the air raid so far in advance is a mystery.

THE FREIBURG DUCK

There is even a case of a duck warning of an air raid. The citizens of Freiburg in Germany were woken up one night in the Second World War by loud quacking as a terrified duck ran through the streets. There was no siren warning of a raid but many people were so alarmed by the duck's panic that they took to their shelters. Soon afterwards the city sustained a heavy bombing that claimed thousands of lives. The survivors were so grateful to the duck they erected a monument in memory of its warning. Perhaps the bird had picked up subtle changes in air pressure in advance of the planes, or maybe it was all just an extraordinary coincidence. We simply don't know.

SALLY

Dogs have given warnings of much smaller-scale impending air disasters. Barbara Duff was living in southern England close to army and air force manoeuvres shortly before the Second World War. Her brother was visiting and their Shetland border collie bitch, Sally, was sleeping in his room when in the early hours of the morning she started panting, whimpering and clawing at him and he could do nothing to settle her. Then about half an hour later a strange noise grew steadily louder. 'Before I could move there was a terrifying thump followed by silence,' said Barbara. A two-seater plane had crashed into their back garden. Fortunately, the crew bailed out safely and the Duff household escaped harm. Perhaps Sally could hear the aircraft was in trouble long before it crashed because she was used to the sound of similar planes.

TOBY

Pets have also rescued their owners from fatal accidents through use of what seem to be paranormal powers. One Sunday evening, mechanic Josef Schwarzl was working on a car in his workshop at San Jose in California with the engine idling. What he didn't realise was that the building's extractor fan had broken and because it was cold he had the garage doors closed. The shop rapidly filled up with deadly carbon monoxide from the exhaust, and Schwarzl slipped into unconsciousness.

Meanwhile, Toby, his golden Labrador, was at home four miles away with Schwarzl's mother. Toby became very agitated and began barking. 'He kept running to the door, scratching wildly at it and when I let him out he headed towards the workshop,' said Mrs Schwarzl. She drove to the garage with a neighbour and discovered Josef slumped inside. 'Somehow Toby knew of the danger that I was in and saved my life,' claimed Josef. But how the dog knew of the danger is a mystery.

Cats and dogs have given warnings of all sorts of other impending disasters. Dr Ute Pleimes, a German psychiatrist at Geissen University, researched over 800 cases of pet warnings of disasters, a high proportion of which were by cats, suggesting perhaps that cats hear sounds or smell things we are unaware of. How these animals can foretell imminent disasters may also be thanks to an extraordinary sense of pressure, which will be discussed in the next section.

WEATHER FORECASTING FAUNA

Animals have long been used to forecast the weather and if you watch cats carefully you can get some very good weather advice. Cats wiping their jaws with their feet, especially passing a paw behind their ears, is a warning sign of rain. They also become less playful before rain, but woe betide you if your cat suddenly becomes frisky. Sailors were said to be very concerned when they saw a cat on board ship being unusually playful or quarrelsome, forecasting a gale. Cats with their tails up and hair apparently electrified indicate approaching wind, and they say that if a cat licks itself with its face turned towards the north, the wind will soon blow from there. According to one correspondent to the *Field* magazine, just before a depression strikes 'our cat runs around the house in a mad fashion, which coincides with low barometric pressure and mercury always falling fast'.

TORNADO CAT

Some cats can also give life-saving warnings about severe weather and there are many stories of cats running around frantically before hurricanes and tornadoes. One Kansas farmer near the town of Lawrence claimed that his cat predicted a tornado well in advance by moving her four kittens from a nearby barn to another farm over a mile away. When the tornado struck it completely destroyed the barn. How she could have known the tornado was going to strike at that spot is a mystery.

REDSEY

Dogs also have a sense of approaching changes in weather. As William Montgomery was preparing to fish off the coast of New England on 10 September 1938, he whistled for his setter Redsey to jump on board as usual. The day was perfect, with hardly a breeze, no clouds, and nothing wrong with the boat. But the dog refused to board, and stood on the dock and barked. Montgomery knew something was wrong for Redsey to behave so out of character, so he stayed in dock. An hour later a tremendous storm suddenly blew up with huge waves, smashing boats and coastal buildings. It was the start of the great hurricane of 1938, which lasted twelve days, killed over 600 people and caused over $250 million of damage. It was also the first hurricane in the region for seventy years, so the experience was unique for any dog living in the area.

Scientists are now beginning to understand more about how animals can predict the weather. Birds can tell when storms are on the way by using a special sort of 'barometer' in their ears, which picks up minute changes in atmospheric pressure. A similar pressure sensor has been discovered in a bat which lives deep in caves and can tell what the weather is like outside. So it's not stretching credibility to imagine that cats and dogs may also pick up approaching storms from changes in the air pressure. This may explain how cats knew of imminent air raids in the Second World War, by picking up changes in pressure or sound. Sound is, after all, simply a change in air pressure.

* * *

EARTH-SHAKING PET WARNINGS

GUNDO

Pets also have extraordinary sensitivity to seismic events. One summer's afternoon, police dog handler Johann Steiner watched from the window of his house near the village of Baldramsdorf in Austria as a massive thunderstorm broke out over the surrounding mountains. His dog Gundo, a seven-year-old Alsatian, was pacing to and fro, whimpering and running to the front door, so he let him out and Gundo dashed off barking. Then above the noise of the storm came a rumble of rocks and the cracking of breaking trees. A mudslide had started high up in the mountains and was heading for his house. Steiner rushed his parents and Gundo into his car and as they drove off their house disappeared under a twenty-foot wall of mud.

EARTHQUAKE ANIMALS

Both pets and wild animals have long had a reputation for predicting earthquakes, going frantic sometimes for days beforehand. But they have only once been used successfully to forecast a quake when in Haicheng, China animals behaved so wildly that the authorities evacuated thousands of people. Forty-eight hours later, on 4 February 1976, the city was devastated by a massive quake. Yet many other cities have had animal warnings and ignored them. Before the Agadir quake in Morocco in 1960 animals were seen fleeing the port before the shock that killed 15,000 people. A quake in the Udine region of northern Italy near the Yugoslav border on 6 May 1976 was heralded by the concerted barking of dogs. In 1979, just south of San Francisco, animals started behaving strangely and erratically at a safari park near the San Andreas Fault, shortly followed by a strong quake.

In the Friuli district of north-eastern Italy, on 6 May 1976, cats and dogs raced backwards and forwards scratching furiously at doors and windows and shortly afterwards the region was struck by a major earthquake. Dr Helmut Tributsch, biochemist at the Max Planck Society's Fritz Haber Institute in Berlin, and originally from the Friuli region, and was amazed to learn all the cats in one village left their homes well before the shock waves hit. This and many other animal phenomena so deeply impressed him he went on to investigate thirty-nine other earthquakes and discovered that pets and wild animals often left their normally safe homes up to a week or more before the quakes struck.

Geologists in America have also looked into animal predictions of quakes. Jim Berkland was county geologist in the Santa Clara district near San Francisco and he was mystified when his normally loyal dog Rocky vanished one day for no apparent reason. Then ten days later a quake hit – Rocky seemed to have known something was wrong, although he didn't return home for another six months.

Then Jim noticed how newspaper adverts for lost cats and dogs would suddenly surge in the days before tremors and quakes hit a region. He could even predict the severity of the disaster because the more animals that went missing and the earlier they disappeared, the larger the quake. For instance, about a week before the massive Los Angeles earthquake of 17 January 1994, fifty-eight dogs were reported missing in the *Los Angeles Times*, which is about double the normal number. But a bigger surge of pet disappearances struck some three to four weeks before the larger 'World Series' quake in San Francisco on 17 October 1989. Jim Berkland also reports other signs before quakes, with big surges in the numbers of stray dogs picked up, more animals run over in roads and dogs howling all night.

How cats and dogs pick up signs of earthquakes where man-made instruments have failed is difficult to explain. One problem is that we still don't understand what happens before a quake, otherwise we might have a reliable way of predicting them. One theory is that bursts of electromagnetic energy precede a quake, as recorded before the quake in Kobe, Japan in January 1995. Some animals may well sense these changes; we know that many creatures are sensitive to magnetism and electricity. Gases such as radon are also thought to be released from the underlying rocks before a quake and animals might be able to smell these. But this is all speculation and illustrates how little we understand both seismic disasters and animal senses.

5

Pet Odysseys

Quite apart from doing brave deeds for people, pets have performed astonishing feats of heroism for themselves, whether using their initiative to find their way back to previous homes, or surviving unimaginable hardships and suffering, or paying homage to their dead owners. There are hundreds of these cases from all over the world and they demonstrate how pets have powers of tenacity, stamina and navigation that we do not fully recognise or understand.

*   *   *

PET TREK

Many wild animals regularly travel the world using breathtaking powers of navigation: birds fly between continents, whales and dolphins swim through the oceans, eels find their way over land and through sea. Far less well appreciated are the fantastic voyages of pets, and their stories highlight yet another heroic and mysterious side to their behaviour.

The stories of epic dog treks are legendary. A collie called Bobbie from Silverton, Oregon went missing while away with his owner in Wolcott, Indiana. Six months and 3,000 miles later he arrived back home bedraggled having crossed major rivers, the Great Plains and the Rocky Mountains of North America. An Alsatian named Barry walked 1,200 miles from southern Italy to the home of his former master in Solingen, West Germany, which took him over a year to complete. Nick, an Alsatian bitch from Selah, Washington got lost while on a camping holiday in the southern Arizona desert, but returned home four months and 2,000 miles later having travelled through deserts, across the Grand Canyon, through blizzards, icy rivers and snow-covered mountain ranges.

There are some remarkable similarities between these stories, suggesting a common way that cats and dogs make their odysseys. At the end of the section we will look at some of the possible explanations for this type of pet phenomenon.

RUSTY

It's not just the distances these dogs covered that are staggering. Some of them also seem to travel amazingly fast. Possibly the world speed record for a pet trek was made in 1949 when a dog named Rusty followed his owner from Boston to Chicago, a distance of 950 miles, in 83 days at an average of over 11 miles per day. Perhaps he hitched rides home somehow.

MICKY

Other dog journeys have been much more modest but no less brave. Micky, a terrier from King's Langley in Hertfordshire, was fifteen-years-old, blind and almost totally deaf when his worries were compounded by the death of his master. He was taken to live with new owners, Mr and Mrs Philips, several miles away at Hemel Hempstead, and stayed there for three years until one Easter he disappeared. Police discovered him outside his old home, which was now derelict, having trekked across busy main roads and a maze of suburban streets, much of it unfamiliar territory.

SANDY

Some pets have used their navigation skills to escape danger. Sandy was a mongrel and mascot of the Royal Signals company based in Alexandria, Egypt during the Second World War. As the British army was driven back by the Germans, Sandy was evacuated with his company to El Alamein. Unfortunately the truck Sandy was travelling in was captured by the Germans. The crew was taken prisoner and Sandy was kicked out. But a few weeks later, Sandy reappeared in Alexandria, having walked across 140 miles of desert in the heat of the day and the cold of the night, in the midst of intense fighting, and then found his way through the labyrinth of city streets to the barracks. He was welcomed as a hero and immediately resumed his position as mascot of his company.

PRINCE

In *Animal War Heroes* (1933), Peter Shaw describes the amazing adventures of Prince, a half terrier, half collie. Prince was so devoted to his owner, James Brown, that he was inconsolable when James left for France at the beginning of the First World War with the 1st North Staffordshire Regiment in 1914. Prince moped for hours, lying with his head in his paws, and finally one day disappeared from his home in Hammersmith, London. He somehow found his way to a Channel port, boarded a transport ship to France and tracked down his master in a trench near Armentières. Private Brown was staggered as Prince leaped on him in excitement. News of the reunion travelled fast and next morning Private Brown had orders to parade his pet before his Commanding Officer. Prince was adopted as the mascot of the regiment and stayed in France throughout the war. Prince's journey turned into a big newspaper story and he became something of a celebrity. The RSPCA investigated the story thoroughly and found it authentic. But how Prince travelled overland, across the English Channel and then found his master in the right trench in France remains a mystery.

TROUBLES

More recently, another war story fits a similar pattern of uncanny canine navigation. During the Vietnam War, dog handler William Richardson was wounded in a jungle skirmish and rushed by helicopter to a field hospital, but his dog, Troubles, was inadvertently left behind. Three weeks later, a thin and exhausted Troubles returned to his headquarters ten miles away from where he was abandoned, and went directly to his master's tent where he rested. How did Troubles find his way back on his own through thick jungle with which he was totally unfamiliar? If Richardson and Troubles had originally walked into the jungle, then it might be explained by the dog following a scent trail home. But as the pair had been taken in by helicopter and Richardson had been lifted out the same way, no scent could have been left on the ground. Troubles's navigation home remains a mystery.

SCOTTISH COLLIE

An even more incredible story concerns a nineteenth-century collie who was sent off by its owner, living near the small port of Inverkeithing in Scotland, to a friend in Calcutta, India. Some time after its arrival in India the dog disappeared and a few months later it bounded into the house of its old master at Inverkeithing, showing great delight to be home again. It had stowed away at Calcutta on a ship bound for Dundee and then taken a coastal vessel to Inverkeithing. It was suggested that the collie had been attracted to the right ship at Calcutta by the Scottish accents of the sailors!

DOG BURGLAR

Pet navigation can land owners in big trouble. In 1990, burglar Dean Mattingly was robbing a house in Oxfordshire with his pet Jack Russell tied on a lead to a post. But when Mattingly was disturbed during the burglary he rushed out, leaving his dog behind. When the police arrived they untied the hapless animal and soon found that it wanted to lead them straight back to his home.

Mattingly was arrested, admitted two charges of burglary and was jailed for fifteen months.

HAINE

Cats also have an impressive track record in navigation skills and endurance. In the autumn of 1977, fourteen-year-old Kirsten Hicks of Adelaide, Australia left his white Persian cat, Haine, with his grandparents over a thousand miles away on Queensland's Gold Coast while he went abroad with his family for a holiday. But when he returned his grandparents broke the news that the cat had disappeared. A year later, Haine turned up on the doorstep of the Hicks' family home in Adelaide, his white coat matted and filthy, paws sore and bloody, but purring. The cat had travelled across rivers, deserts and vast wilderness in an amazing twelve-month trek to get home.

TOM

Most cases of pet navigation concern animals returning to their homes, but there are much more mysterious cases of animals trekking to completely unfamiliar destinations. In 1949 Mr and Mrs Charles B. Smith moved to San Gabriel, California from St Petersburgh, Florida. They left their cat Tom with the new owner, Robert Hanson, but two weeks after the Smiths moved he wrote to say that Tom had run away. Then one afternoon, just over two years later in early August 1951, Mr and Mrs Smith noticed a cat wailing in the yard. It ran towards Mr Smith and although the cat was now very skinny, frazzled and his paws bloody, he was convinced it was Tom.

SUGAR

Incredible feats of pet navigation are often explained as a case of mistaken identity – a different animal being mistaken for the lost pet. But one convincing case, a positive identification of a lost pet, was a cream-coloured Persian cat called Sugar, who trailed his owners across 1,500 miles to a place it had never been to before. In 1951 Sugar's family moved from Andersen, California at the northern end of the Sacramento Valley, to Gage, Oklahoma. But the cat refused to get into the car and was left with neighbours. Shortly afterwards Sugar disappeared. Fourteen months later he turned up at the Smith's new home in an emaciated state, but overjoyed to see his family again and they too were ecstatic at the reunion. The Smiths knew it was the same cat because he had a clear deformity of the left hip. But how he crossed a desert, several canyons and the Rocky Mountains remains a mystery.

NEW YORK VET

Another case of proven identity of a lost pet was related by Michael Fox in *Understanding Your Cat* (1974). A New York vet left his cat in his home state while he went to take up a post in California 2,500 miles away. Months later an identical cat walked into his new house. Amazed to see his old friend again the vet examined the animal and found the tell-tale deformed bone growth on the fourth vertebra of its tail that had identified his cat – there was no question of mistaken identity.

PITCHON

There is even a case of a pet cat being sighted during a marathon journey. When Fernand Schmitt went away by train from his home in Merlebach to join the French army, his kitten Pitchon was left behind with a neighbour. But Pitchon ran away, travelling seventy-five miles through the Vosges mountains, arriving bedraggled eleven days later at the army barracks in Strasbourg where Fernand was sleeping. Fernand was so surprised to see his kitten again he tried to find out how it had got to him. He traced railway workers who had seen the kitten walking along the railway tracks and two army officers who had witnessed her arrival at Strasbourg. If indeed they had seen the same kitten it seems as if she had traced her owner's journey, but we're at a loss to explain how.

ALFIE

Some pets are such good navigators they can even find their way home on their own by public transport! In March 1995, a border collie called Alfie was left outside a card shop in Plymouth while his owner, Laura Knight, browsed inside for a few moments. But when she came out he had disappeared – Alfie had trotted down the road to a bus stop, waited, and caught a number twenty-one bus to his home at the Lyneham Inn at Plympton in Devon. But the journey didn't quite go according to plan. The bus driver wouldn't let him get off because he was afraid for the dog's safety, so he took him to the police station where Laura later collected him. 'I couldn't believe it. Alfie's always been a bit crazy but this was amazing,' she told the local newspaper. 'It's so clever of him to get on the right bus even if he did drive me mad with worry.' It was even more astonishing that he got on the bus going in the right direction and knew when to get off.

TRAIN-TRAVELLING TERRIER

Edwin Arnold, in his book *The Soul of the Beast* (1960), tells of a dog which found its way back to its old home by train, and even changed trains en route. Mr A. E. Dowden had an English wire-haired terrier who slipped out of his house shortly before 6 p.m. one Monday evening. There was no trace of him until his old landlady in Staines over twenty miles away rang to say the dog had arrived at her doorstep. Meanwhile, a railway guard had seen the dog jumping into a carriage on a train at the local station at Bishop's Road. The canine commuter got off at West Croydon and changed platforms for the train to Staines, got off at the correct station and then walked the rest of the way to his old landlady's house. Only once had he made the same train journey, a fortnight beforehand, suggesting that dogs have astounding memories for travel routes.

TIBS, THE TRAIN-CATCHING CAT

Cats have also taken train journeys on their own initiative. Tibs was the station cat at Preston but when she became pregnant she decided that a change of scenery was needed. Tibs jumped onto a train to London and got off at Euston station, perhaps needing the anonymity of the big city to start a new life. Unfortunately for her she was caught by an alert porter who read the address tag on her collar and Tibs was sent home under escort.

BADGER AND TANGO

Horses, too, have their own homing instincts. Badger and Tango had lived most of their lives in a field at Skirmett, Buckinghamshire but when their owner, Julia Orr, moved house she took them to a new paddock. Six weeks later a storm blew open the gate to the horses' field and they seized their chance to escape and disappeared. Julia was distraught until she got a call from her previous home to say that her two horses had been found at dawn at the gate of their old field waiting to be let in. Badger and Tango had walked nine miles along a busy road, at night, through unfamiliar territory, and in the right direction until they arrived at what they considered to be their real home.

HARRY THE TORTOISE

Even the slower members of the animal kingdom can manage their own mammoth treks. Harry the tortoise plodded home eight miles in four days to be reunited with his owner after getting lost on a trip to the vet in October 1992. Pensioner Stuart Gray found his pet on the doorstep after he lost the fifteen-year-old tortoise while taking him for a health check-up at Ryde on the Isle of Wight. He had put down Harry's box when he met a friend, but while his back was turned the tortoise had tipped the box over and disappeared.

Pets have uncanny powers of navigation, even using public transport. Tibs the cat fled Preston by catching a train to London, but was escorted home again when she was discovered without a ticket. (Syndication International Ltd)

TOPA THE HEDGEHOG

According to a report from the Soviet news agency TASS in 1979, a hedgehog named Topa went on a mammoth trek back to a vet. Topa had been found on a country road with a broken paw by veterinary doctor Nadezhda Ushakova, who set the paw and then gave the hedgehog to her granddaughter who took it home to Dimitrov forty-eight miles away. But soon afterwards the granddaughter said that Topa had refused to eat and became very sluggish, so she took it to a nearby forest and set it free. Two months later, Dr Ushakova found Topa sitting on her doorstep when she returned home from work. The hedgehog was in good health despite having travelled at the ferocious pace of just under a mile a day.

PIGEON NUMBER 167

Birds are probably the most extraordinary pet navigators. In autumn 1939, twelve-year-old Hugh Brady Perkins of Summerville, West Virginia befriended an exhausted homing pigeon and named it Billy. A few months later Hugh was taken to hospital in Phillipi, West Virginia, 120 miles from his home. One snowy night, about a week after his arrival, Hugh heard a fluttering at the window of his hospital room. He called a nurse and told her there was a bird trying to get in. To keep him happy she opened the window, and a pigeon hopped in. Hugh immediately recognised it as Billy and told the nurse to look for an identity ring on its leg carrying the number 167, and it was there. When his parents came to visit a few days later, they confirmed that it was indeed his bird. It hadn't been brought with them, and neither could it have followed the family car. Somehow the pigeon succeeded in flying 120 miles and locating the correct window in a building it had never seen before, in a strange town at night and in a snowstorm. And how did it even know that Hugh was there? It is a mystery.

HOW DO THEY DO THAT?

Animals navigate using a range of different senses. Whales, birds, bees and many other animals sense the earth's magnetic field, which tells them direction, distance, altitude, or even depth in water. They combine this with direction readings from the sun and perhaps even the stars. An exact location can be pinpointed with visual landmarks and a strong sense of smell, combined with a powerful memory for reading the landscape. Scientists found that racing pigeons can find their way home even when fitted with frosted contact lenses, preventing them looking for visual landmarks.

These are skills we know about in wild animals, but far less is known about pet navigation. Experiments in the 1920s showed that cats released into unfamiliar surroundings turned in the correct direction and made the shortest return route home, even when they had been transported in boxes or doped to prevent them making mental maps of the route. Biologist Dr Rupert Sheldrake in London is now hoping to find out how dogs navigate by taking them into unfamiliar territory and using satellite navigation devices to pinpoint their route home. Although his research is still in its early stages, the first results seem to show that a dog will wander around apparently at random for some time, perhaps trying to get its bearings, before setting off on a determined route back home. This does not yet answer the question, how do cats and dogs find their way over great distances and sometimes over strange territory? Like wild animals they may have some sort of inbuilt compass, a sense of the earth's magnetism, and use smell and visual cues. But this still can not explain how they sometimes find their way to owners at unfamiliar destinations, like Sugar the cat or Prince the dog, for example. And neither does it say anything about the determination which drives them to make such heroic odysseys.

ENDURANCE BEYOND BELIEF

We often underestimate the stamina of many pets and their will to survive in appalling conditions and despite suffering unbelievable pain.

BRUNO

When Andrew and Merrill Pitts lost their cat Bruno over Easter 1996, they searched high and low for him in their house, garden and neighbourhood but without luck. The four-year-old pet was a loyal character and had never wandered far before, but eventually the couple were resigned to him being lost forever. Then six weeks later, builders converting a house two doors away heard a faint miaowing from under the floorboards. They found an emaciated Bruno, who had survived for forty-five days in the dark, probably by eating spiders and licking condensation off pipes under the boards. He had lost half his bodyweight and was put on a dripfeed by a vet before he recovered.

TABITHA

Quite a few cats have had traumatic experiences on aircraft. On 1 July 1994 a three-year-old tabby cat called Tabitha became lost inside a jumbo jet after escaping from its carrier in the cargo hold. Passengers could hear faint noises from underneath the first class section but attempts to find her failed, despite using electronic machinery and tuna bait. The plane went on to fly from New York to Puerto Rico to Los Angeles and on to Miami – a distance of 30,000 miles – but there was still no sign of Tabitha. Pleas by Tabitha's owner, Carol Timmel, to ground the aircraft for a proper search went unheeded until she threatened a court injunction on the airline, Tower Air. Eventually she found the cat alive in the aircraft's rear ceiling panel behind the passenger compartment and, despite the terrifying ordeal, Tabitha recovered fully.

FELIX

Another cat suffered an even worse marathon ordeal in the cargo hold of a jumbo jet, after squeezing out of her box on a journey from California to Frankfurt. Four-year-old Felix spent a month as a stowaway, clocking up 279,900 miles all over the world, touching down in locations such as Los Angeles, Miami, St Maarten in the Caribbean, Rio de Janeiro, Paris and Riyadh in Saudi Arabia, amongst a total of sixty-four destinations. She emerged emaciated on New Year's Day 1988 after surviving on condensed water drops on the sides of the cargo section. Pan Am staff traced her owners in London, and they were overjoyed to find Felix still alive. They were less enthusiastic about the automatic quarantine she had to endure at Heathrow Airport, because of Britain's strict anti-rabies laws.

LOUISE AND CAPTAIN GRAVENEY

Perhaps the most horrific experience of any animal on a plane was when a cat was almost cooked alive in flight. In November 1995, British Airways flight BA224 from Houston to London had been flying for two hours when the captain discovered that the cargo hold was overheating because of a faulty thermostat. The temperature had risen to 55°C (131°F), equivalent to a hot day in Kuwait. Amongst the cargo was a small cat, Louise, who Captain Graveney guessed would eventually die in the heat. He asked the 200 passengers on board to vote whether or not to detour and make an emergency stop at Boston to save the cat, or to continue as scheduled. Almost all of them raised their hands in agreement to save Louise. When the flight landed at Boston, a very dehydrated Louise was taken off but after cooling down and taking liquids she slowly regained her normal composure. The flight eventually arrived at London's Gatwick Airport three hours late and cost British Airways £12,000 in extra fuel, but Captain Graveney insisted he'd done the right thing: 'We would have diverted if a passenger had been taken ill, so I thought why not do it for someone who can't talk?' He was later

Felix, the globe-trotting cat, endured a month aboard an aircraft before she was discovered barely alive, having survived by licking moisture off the sides of the cargo hold. (Rex Features Ltd)

awarded a medal for compassion to animals by the World Society for the Protection of Animals (WSPA).

COCONUT HARRY

Dogs have had even more hair-raising adventures than lost cats. Naomi Simoneli was out on a boat off the Florida coast with her four-year-old golden Labrador, Coconut Harry, when the weather deteriorated and a huge wave suddenly knocked him off the boat into the sea. Naomi and a flotilla of rescue boats searched the area extensively but without success, and she returned home depressed but determined not to give up hope. Next day she started distributing hundreds of posters and made appeals in the local press and radio for any information on Harry's whereabouts. Eight days later, research scientists made one of their fortnightly trips to an island populated by resident Rhesus monkeys and found the apes screaming mad for no apparent reason, until they spotted Harry trotting around the island. He must have swam five miles to get to the island, an extraordinary feat of stamina for any dog and especially in such heavy seas.

FLOSS

An astonishing ordeal was suffered by a sheepdog called Floss, who was trying to find a stray goose during a blizzard when she was blown over a cliff at Whitby in Yorkshire. Her owner, Will Lewis, was devastated and feared her dead but unknown to him she had landed on a rock outcrop forty feet below and was only discovered ten days later by a passerby looking up from the beach. Will Lewis immediately ran to the rescue and was hauled up by rope sixty feet from the bottom of the cliff until he found Floss stranded on a narrow shale ledge. She had survived snow, sleet, wind and cold, without food or water, suffered broken legs and was reduced to skin and bone. 'Floss was very hoarse because she had probably been barking all the time but no one could hear her,' said Mr Lewis. He thought she survived by licking moisture from the damp shale.

STICKEEN

The famous American naturalist, John Muir, went on an expedition to Alaska in the summer of 1880 to explore glaciers, guided by a party of Stickeen indians in a canoe and a small dog also called Stickeen. The dog was very independent and strong, and when Muir decided to go exploring alone on the glacier the dog followed him. They walked across the glacier, both of them jumping over small crevasses. But eventually they arrived at one particularly large crevasse that was so wide the only way across was via a thin ice bridge. It was getting too late to retrace their steps, so Muir cut steps into the ice bridge and crawled across on his knees. Stickeen was very reluctant to follow but seeing the situation was desperate he at last lay down and pressed his body against the ice to get a grip, put his feet together, sliding them down into the next step, working his way over the ice. Dogs are poor climbers but Stickeen crawled up the sides of the ice bridge on the other side of the crevasse by hooking his paws into the notches and steps, and eventually made it across. According to Muir, when the little dog finally got across he ran around yelping with joy.

* * *

ESCAPE

EMILY

One heartwarming story stands out from all others. Emily the cow, a three-year-old Holstein heifer, was about to walk to the slaughterhouse in Hopkinton, Massachusetts on 14 November 1995 when her survival instincts drove her to make a five-foot leap over a holding-pen fence, and she escaped into the woods outside town. There she went grazing with a herd of deer, appeared at a nearby farm and even passed into downtown Hopkinton, but evaded all attempts to capture her for several days. Emily's heroic efforts turned her into a local heroine, and people started leaving her hay in their fields and backyards. Eventually she was rescued by a vegetarian couple, Meg and Lewis Randa, who bought her from her original owner and made her a pet for their local school.

ZARO AND JIRO

In central Tokyo there is a statue of a pair of dogs, commemorating one of the most outstanding feats of animal endurance ever known. The dogs were part of a pack of fifteen huskies sent to the South Pole as sleigh dogs for two expeditions in 1956 and 1958. But after the expeditions the base was closed and the dogs were left in Antarctica over winter with impossibly small chances of survival. The following year, in 1959, the same members of the expedition returned not expecting to find any surviving dogs, but were astounded to find that two of them were still alive. Zaro and Jiro recognised the men and rushed to greet them. They were taken back to Hoccaido in Japan where their heroic survival became a national legend. The statue was erected in their honour at the base of Tokyo Tower.

*   *   *

BEST FRIENDS

Of all pets, dogs have an amazing loyalty to their owners, probably born out of their natural instinct – already described in the book – to follow the leader of the pack.

TRUFFLES

Earlier on we saw that dogs will very often instinctively stay by an owner in trouble, but this loyalty can be disastrous if help needs to be called. In one case, though, a spaniel who stayed by her owner's side saved her life thanks to the dog's loyalty and reflective eyes. One afternoon in December 1990, Joyce Harris had been out walking

Truffles saved her owner Joyce Harris after she had fallen outdoors by staying with her and keeping her warm. Eventually a rescue helicopter found the pair at night thanks to Truffles's eyes reflecting their searchlight. (Torbay News Agency)

Truffles near their home at Dunsford in Devon when she tripped, hit her head and fell unconscious in a field. After a while, her husband, Tom, grew anxious and search parties with tracker dogs were sent out to find her, but they turned back as it grew dark. Only a police helicopter could carry on the search. When the crew picked out Truffles's eyes shining out in their searchlight, seventy-four-year-old Joyce was found beside her, unharmed except for concussion thanks to Truffles lying by her side and keeping her warm.

AIRCRAFT-SPOTTING COCKER

Dogs recognise their owners and their vehicles, but a correspondent to *The Field* magazine wrote from Somerset that he had a golden cocker spaniel who recognised his aircraft. In the 1950s, when he was flying jet-fighter aircraft in Norfolk, the dog spent a lot of time with him on airfields and was quite at home there waiting for him. About five minutes before he was due to land at the end of each sortie the dog would suddenly get up and beg for the door to be opened, and wait by the flight line. As the aircraft taxied in – sometimes as many as eight at a time and in a different order from takeoff – he would dash up to the one his master was flying, always meeting the right one and taking care to keep clear until the engines were running down.

RUSWARP

The bond between dog and owner can be so close that many dogs stand guard over their dead masters. On 20 January 1990, Graham Nuttall left his home for a weekend's walking in the Elan Valley in Wales, accompanied by his fourteen-year-old cross border collie called Ruswarp. When he failed to return home, friends alerted the police who searched the area but couldn't find him. Some three months later, on 7 April 1990, Ruswarp was found collapsed and starving on a remote hill in mid-Wales by a rambler who also found the body of Graham Nuttall nearby. Ruswarp had stayed by his dead master for three months and was so weak that he had to be carried down from the hills.

HACHIKO

An even more dramatic display of loyalty was given by Hachiko, a Japanese Akito dog belonging to Dr Eisaburo Ueno, who worked at Tokyo University. Hachiko walked with his master every day to Shibuya railway station in Tokyo and returned there every night to greet him. Then one day in 1925, Dr Ueno died suddenly whilst at the university, but that night Hachiko was at the station as usual and waited in vain for his master until midnight. He returned the next night at the same time, and then every night for the next ten years until eventually dying in 1935. Local people had noticed the dog's loyalty over the years and were so deeply touched they erected a small bronze statue in memory of Hachiko at the station, and every year on 8 April a special ceremony is held in honour of the dog.

GREYFRIARS BOBBY

Greyfriars Bobby's is probably the most famous story of dog loyalty. Bobby was a black Skye terrier working with his shepherd Auld Jock, who herded sheep on Cauldbrae Farm in the Pentland Hills in southern Scotland. Every Wednesday they both went to market day in Edinburgh and at exactly 1p.m. would go for lunch at Traill's Dining Rooms in Greyfriars Place nearby. Despite it being busy on a market day, the owner, John Traill, always spoke to Auld Jock with Bobby at his heels.

Then one day in 1858 Jock was sacked from his job. Jock was driven back to Edinburgh Grassmarket to get him well away from the farm where he was unwanted, and presumably away from Bobby as well. But Bobby knew something was wrong and set off back to Edinburgh Grassmarket on his own, eventually finding Jock in a dirty passageway. The two of them spent the night in a seedy lodging house in Cowgate and slept on straw in the attic, but next day Jock could not be raised – he was dead. When he was buried

The world's most famous loyal dog was Greyfriars Bobby, who visited his dead master's grave daily for fourteen years. The people of Edinburgh were so moved by Bobby's devotion he was given the freedom of the city and commemorated with this memorial. (The Still Moving Picture Company)

in nearby Greyfriars churchyard, the *Scotsman* newspaper reported, 'the dog, a Scotch terrier, was one of the most conspicuous mourners'.

Three days after the funeral, at exactly 1p.m., John Traill was taken aback when Bobby walked into the Dining Rooms half-starved, looking for food. He gave him a bone and the dog left. But Bobby returned the next day and this time John Traill followed him when he left and discovered him at the churchyard. He took Bobby back to his old farmer at Cauldbrae Farm, but soon afterwards the dog ran away again to the graveyard and, even though various people including John Traill tried to adopt him, Bobby howled until allowed back to Greyfriars churchyard. News spread of the terrier's extraordinary loyalty to the graveside of his dead shepherd – children fussed over him and people gathered outside the graveyard gates to watch the dog leave each day just before 1p.m. to go to Traill's Dining Rooms for food.

For nine years this routine continued until the local authorities decided the law was being broken. Bobby was taken to court for being unlicensed and was declared a 'vagrant'. Traill was imprisoned for 'harbouring' him, although the charge was later dismissed. The day after the court hearing, Bobby's whole story was reported in the *Scotsman* under the heading, 'Strange Story of Dog', and when the Lord Provost of Edinburgh, William Chambers, read the article he adopted Bobby himself, paid his licence fee and gave him the freedom of the city and a new collar inscribed 'Greyfriars Bobby, from the Lord Provost, 1867 – licensed!'

There was no further news of Bobby until January 1872, when the *Scotsman* carried an obituary for him: 'Many will be sad to hear that the poor but interesting dog, Greyfriars Bobby, died on Sunday evening. Every kind attention was paid to him in his last days by his guardian, Mr Traill, who has had him buried in a flower plot near Greyfriars Church'. A memorial statue of Greyfriars Bobby was commissioned and still stands today above a drinking fountain on the corner of Candlemaker Row and George VI Bridge, and his special collar given by the Lord Provost is in the Huntly House Museum in Canongate. The grave of his master is now marked by a headstone erected by Bobby's American admirers, and although Mr Traill's Dining Rooms no longer exists it is commemorated at number 6, Greyfriars Place with a brass plate on the door which reads, 'Greyfriars Bobby was fed here 1858–1872'.

ZORRO

If a dog's owner suddenly disappears, the dog will very often wait at the last place they were both together, sometimes with heartrending consequences. In 1975 Mark Cooper left his home in California on a trip to Sierra Nevada with his faithful dog Zorro, a German shepherd. While walking in the mountains, Mark lost his balance and toppled into a ravine, falling eighty-five feet. He was knocked out and landed in a stream below. As he slowly regained consciousness he became aware of Zorro trying to pull him out of the water and up a steep rocky slope. Mark was later found by friends who went to get help while Zorro lay on top of him and kept him warm. Next day a helicopter was brought in and Mark was winched to safety, but unfortunately Zorro was forgotten and left behind. Days later he was spotted by walkers, guarding Mark's backpack as if waiting for his master to return in a touching display of loyalty. He was honoured in 1976 with the American Dog Hero of the Year Award.

BEES

Bees are not usually considered pets but they do show a very impressive loyalty to their keepers, and there is an old country saying that when beekeepers die their bees come to pay their last respects at the funeral. Several cases of this have been recorded, including one recent one in Ludlow, a market town in Shropshire.

Margaret Bell was a keen beekeeper all her life and loved bees so much she even talked to them. When she died in June 1994 the mourners leaving her funeral service were walking down to her house when hundreds of her bees swarmed through the town centre in such a thick cloud that people took shelter and car drivers wound up their windows. 'We couldn't believe it when we heard the bees coming down the street. They turned the sky dark,' said Sue Walsh, a friend of Margaret's. The bees then settled on a building directly opposite Margaret's house and stayed there for about an hour while the mourners remained inside Margaret's home, then flew off over the rooftops and disappeared.

6

Pets Rescue Pets

You could argue that pets can behave heroically because it is in their best interests to save their owners who give them food and shelter. But many animals risk their lives for purely altruistic reasons – for other animals. This section features tales that show the enormous courage of mothers where their offspring are concerned. But more extraordinary yet are animals who have rescued unrelated creatures, even animals of a different species. It's these animal rescues that paint another side to pet heroism.

*　*　*

MOTHERS TO THE RESCUE

SCARLETT

Scarlett the stray cat gained worldwide attention after carrying her four-week-old kittens one by one out of a burning building in Brooklyn, New York. She had set up home for her brood in an abandoned garage, but shortly after 6 a.m. on 29 March 1996, the fire service was called out to the building. Firefighter David Gianelli said he could hear the sound of cat cries while fighting the blaze. When the fire was out he went to investigate and discovered three kittens right outside the building, another half way across the street and a fifth on the sidewalk opposite. The kittens were far too small to have pulled themselves out of the burning building on their own, and their burns were progressively more severe, as if the first kittens had been pulled out just as the blaze broke out and the rest had to be carried through the building as the fire grew worse. Gianelli then found the mother collapsed nearby. Her eyes were swollen shut, her paw pads badly burned and her face, ears and legs scorched. She had almost died in order to save her kittens. Gianelli drove the mother and her kittens to the North Shore Animal League sanctuary in New York, where the family was cared for by vets and eventually recovered. Their exploits became news across the world and some 2,000 requests were made to adopt Scarlett and her kittens, from as far away as Japan and the Netherlands. Scarlett also became a star of television news and the Oprah Winfrey Show, and when the North Shore Animal League set up a Scarlett Fund they collected more than $15,000 to help her and future cats in need.

HOG WASH

Although not strictly about a pet, this story is strikingly similar to that of Scarlett. In August 1994, a mother hog was removed from her burning pen during a fire in Leominster, Massachusetts. But she repeatedly returned to the pen until all of her piglets were discovered and rescued. The mother returned to the fire five times, scorching her own skin in the process and she had to be hosed down in between rescue missions by firemen until all the piglets were safe. Pigs are much more sociable and intelligent than we give them credit for. The mother hog's courage was typical of female pigs, who in the wild live in maternal groups with their piglets, feeding and protecting each other against any outside threat.

BEAUTY

Horses have also made life-saving rescues. A mare called Beauty saved the lives of her four-day-old foal and another horse when both fell into the Jan du Toits River in Rawsonville in the Cape of South Africa in September 1993. The river was swollen after days of heavy rain and the foal fell into the torrent when the riverbank collapsed. Then the other horse, Hank Gorter, was swept along by the current, possibly as he was trying to reach the foal. But Beauty jumped into the water and pushed both of them to safety. She was given the South African Society for the Prevention of Cruelty to Animals' bravery award, one of the few occasions a horse has received a medal for heroism in peacetime.

* * *

PETS RESCUE THEIR OWN KIND

'Dog rescues dog' sounds a bizarre sort of rescue mission, but animals brought up with each other often strike up such close relationships that when one is in trouble the other risks life and limb to jump to the other's rescue. This is particularly true of dogs, probably because of their natural instinct to help members of their own pack.

TESSA AND SASHA

Retired engineer Alex Roebuck was out walking with his two dogs, a six-year-old crossbred called Tessa and three-year-old Sasha, a Siberian husky, one cold February day in 1996. Tessa was chasing some ducks on to the frozen Chesterfield Canal when the ice suddenly cracked open under her weight, plunging her into the freezing water. She was thrashing around, fighting for her life, when Sasha leaped off the canal bank, her weight and momentum breaking through the ice. She grabbed Tessa by the scruff of her neck and dragged her twenty feet to the bank, where Alex Roebuck dragged them both out. 'To see the way she responded to the crisis, without a thought for her own safety, brought a lump to my throat,' said Mr Roebuck of Charborough, near Retford, Nottinghamshire. 'Huskies are renowned for their intelligence and rescue feats but I've never heard of one saving another dog.' Sasha's motive for the rescue was probably that Tessa had acted as her adopted mother when she arrived at the Roebuck home as a puppy. Sasha was later awarded an RSPCA bravery medal.

TARKA AND POPPY

When Julie Webb was out with her neighbour Sue Scrafield walking their dogs, neither could have anticipated the drama that followed. They were passing along the banks of the Old Bedford river in Norfolk on 15 February 1995 with the two dogs playing with each other: Tarka, Julie's Labrador, and Poppy, Sue's Yorkshire terrier puppy. Then suddenly Sue turned in horror as she saw Poppy lose her footing, fall into the freezing cold water, and being swept away in the river, which was swollen by recent heavy rainfall. As Poppy disappeared in the raging waters, Tarka immediately jumped into the river after her and now Julie watched in despair as her dog also vanished under the water. Then after several heart-stopping moments, Tarka popped up with the terrier in her mouth and brought her back to the bank alive and well. She was awarded the PRO Dog gold medal award for bravery, 1995.

BO AND HUEY

We have seen how dogs have fallen over cliffs and, after horrendous suffering, been saved by their owners. But injured animals have also been rescued by other pets. On New Year's Day, 1987, Peter Sparks was taking his dogs, Bo and Huey, for a walk by Portishead Cliffs near Bristol, when Bo suddenly plunged seventy feet down the cliffs and lay injured on a ledge on the cliff face. Without a moment's hesitation Huey crawled after him down the cliff by weaving a path through the rocks, until he reached Bo. Then he helped him down to safety, having to push him much of the way because of Bo's injuries and exhaustion. Bo was rushed for emergency treatment at a vet's clinic and eventually recovered fully.

Labrador Tarka heroically threw herself into a raging river to rescue her friend Poppy, a Yorkshire terrier, who had accidentally fallen into the water. (David Paton)

PEKE AND JAMES

Although a dog's natural instinct is to stay with an injured person, sometimes dogs act as companions for other dogs in need. James

93

was a handsome Peke with a great friend next door called Bess, a rather ageing Boxer. One day, owner Fiona Forde could not find James and neither could her next door neighbour Margaret find Bess. The next morning Margaret asked Fiona if she realised that James had been sitting at the end of a ditch at the bottom of their garden for some twenty-four hours. When Fiona went to investigate she found James standing above poor Bess, who was lying below in the ditch having been knocked down by a car. James seemed to be keeping vigil over his friend, who was taken off for emergency treatment and eventually recovered completely.

COWS TO THE RESCUE

This particular story is not about pets but about farm animals. In *Just Like An Animal* (1978), Maurice Burton describes how in 1976 Mr M. E. Purchase was walking along a country road when he saw a new-born calf on a steeply sloping field. As he stopped to look, the calf began to slide helplessly down the grassy hill. The mother gave a strange cry and at once six other cows ran and stood in a line on the hill to stop the calf sliding any further. Having mounted a concerted and successful rescue effort, they all stood around and helped the mother to lick it clean.

* * *

HELP BETWEEN SPECIES

An even more intriguing aspect of pet-rescuing-pet heroics is when different species are involved. Sometimes there is a rational, even biological explanation as to why members of one species should risk their lives for another species, but in other cases it is simply a mystery.

GINNY

According to *Eva* magazine, Ginny the dog was obsessed with rescuing cats and in five years her owner, Philip Gonzalez, witnessed her going to extraordinary lengths to save them in New York. Among her many exploits, she rescued a paralysed cat found on the floor of an empty building and carried her to safety in her mouth; she sniffed out five abandoned kittens left for dead in the bottom of an eight-foot deep pipe in an old warehouse; she cut her paws digging through broken glass to find an abandoned stray in a glass factory. Philip Gonzalez realised Ginny was special from the moment he first got her from an animal shelter: 'We were out walking one night when she ran up to a young alley cat and started rubbing noses with her,' he said. It could be that she was so closely brought up with cats that she thought she was one of them.

SOUTH AFRICAN HEN

Colesberg town in Cape Province, South Africa is in a semi-desert, mostly sheep farming area known as the Karoo. Mrs E. Ingledew describes in *True Stories About Animals and Birds* (1981) how a farming friend of hers had a mother hen with chicks which were being stolen by some sort of a predator during the night. Eventually, only three chicks were left. The mother hen became so exasperated that she took her remaining brood out of the hen coop and into the family dog's kennel, where she lay at the back with her surviving chicks under her wings and the dog lying in front. The dog didn't seem to mind in the least and never raised a paw to hurt them, which probably makes both the mother hen and the dog joint heroes together. The hen was defending her family like any mother would, and because the dog grew up with them he probably saw the birds as honorary canines.

BIRD-LOVING DOG AND CAT

In the cases so far we can explain why one animal helps another species because they were brought up together. But there are two very intriguing stories of cats helping birds that seem to defy this rule. The Jesse family of Shelby Township, Michigan nursed a robin back to health after a storm had left it stranded on their doorstep. When the bird recovered it enjoyed the Jesse household so much it stayed in the house and took such a liking to their Doberman pinscher it would even rest on top of his head.

In a very similar story, in 1957 the American National Cat Food Company awarded a heroine's medal to Minnie, a Siamese cat from Boston, who decided not to make a meal of a pigeon it discovered with a broken leg, but brought it home in her mouth to her owner, Joseph Menex.

NIPPER

In *Heroic Dogs* (1990), Lesley Scott-Ordish writes of a farm dog called Nipper who made a rescue above and beyond the call of duty. In February 1985, Nipper's flock of some 300 ewes and their new lambs were shut inside their barn for the night on Ansty Farm in West Sussex, while everyone had gone to bed. But in the early hours Nipper started barking uncontrollably. By the time farmworkers Patrick and Jayne Leaney were aroused, smoke was pouring out of the barn and the ewes and their lambs were bleating in panic. As soon as they opened the barn door the sheep raced out, but Nipper rushed into the smoke and flames and searched out those sheep who were still trapped inside.

Despite suffering burnt paws and smoke-filled lungs, Nipper repeatedly went back into the burning barn. The situation was made even worse by many of the rescued ewes running back into the barn to search for their lambs still trapped inside. In this mayhem Nipper raced through the thick smoke until he had found all the ewes and lambs. Only ten were killed. But he still wasn't finished. He then went in to rescue cows and calves left at the furthest end of the barn and drove them out as well. For this amazing feat of bravery Nipper was awarded the PRO Dogs Award for devotion in December 1985. 'Self-preservation is the strongest instinct in any animal,' commented Lesley Scott-Ordish, 'and there is no way of ordering a dog to face such a life-threatening situation. It has to have a very high degree of courage.'

CREAM DEE

Cows are not well known for their rescue talents, but Cream Dee became the heroine of her herd on the Isle of Wight when she led her farmer to his lost dog. After five days of searching for his missing Jack Russell terrier, Scally, farmer Malcolm Dyer had all but given up finding him. He had checked all the rabbit holes on the farm in case the dog had chased a rabbit, and still there was no sign of Scally. Then he noticed something strange about Cream Dee. She was standing alone from the rest of the dairy herd beside a hole, ears pricked up and head to one side. On approaching, Malcolm heard a faint whimpering from inside an old badger set. He took his spade, dug deep, and found Scally trapped inside, cold and thirsty but alive. A very rare case of a cow saving a dog.

*   *   *

FOSTER MOTHERS

Pets can sometimes come to the rescue of other animals by using their mothering instincts to foster them. In a few cases they make the oddest of couples in what might be considered weird identity crises.

MEG

Meg was a dog who had lived on a farm with many other animals since she was a puppy but was fascinated by baby guinea-pigs and chickens, which she would round up if they started to stray. As if that didn't keep her well occupied, Meg had an even stranger relationship with three ducklings who would follow her everywhere. When Meg lay down the ducklings would run up between her front paws and she would lick them. As they got older she would round them up for her owner Susan Yoffe by running in front of them and guiding them in the right direction, or gently pushing them with a paw.

PEDRO

Male dogs have made good foster parents, too. Pedro, a Pyrenean Mountain dog took on the role of the nursery rhyme 'Mary Had A Little Lamb' when he adopted a week-old orphaned lamb, for everywhere that Pedro went the little lamb was sure to go. They played together, went for walks together, washed together and even slept together at their home at Heathfield in Sussex. The lamb took to the dog very well after its mother had died.

SOPHIE

Similar sorts of cat fostering have cropped up elsewhere. The RSPCA branch in Cardiff were looking after a stray cat called Sophie and her kitten when they were given a couple of orphaned baby squirrels only a few days old to care for. Having no female squirrel to foster them they tried out Sophie as a surrogate mother and she and her kitten immediately accepted them. Sophie fed them her own milk and the squirrels thrived, clinging to Sophie's belly with their claws and causing her some pain which she put up with stoically.

KITTY WIMPLE

This sort of cat fostering arrangement is not that unusual. Television news broadcaster Martyn Lewis lists quite a few other oddball combinations in his book *Cats in the News* (1991). In Miami, Mr and Mrs Polak took in a young, abandoned sparrow and their cat, Kitty Wimple, was so taken with the bird it shared its food and played with it. Two puppies, which had been rescued from a frozen pond on Clapham Common in London, were given a home where they shared a basket and food with a cat. In Hamburg, a baby

Pedro, a Pyrenean Mountain dog, took on the role of the nursery rhyme 'Mary Had A Little Lamb' when he adopted a week-old lamb. (Fox Photos Ltd)

hedgehog was adopted by a family cat, Leischa, maybe as a substitute for two of her kittens who had just been found new homes. Another German cat fostered three baby hedgehogs found on a farm near Alt-Ötting. A Danish cat fostered a squirrel with her own milk. And when Duchesse – a cat in St Jean-St Maurice in the Loire region of France – had her kittens given away soon after birth, she fostered a baby rabbit with her own milk.

Perhaps weirdest of all, Lesley Scott-Ordish in *Heroic Dogs* (1990) features a case of fostering which is remarkable because it seems so dangerous. Kalli, a crossbred collie bitch, fostered a whole succession of exotic animals at a wildlife park in Northamptonshire, including a puma, a leopard, two lion cubs, and two Arctic fox cubs. Kalli was made PRO Dogs pet of the year in 1980.

7

War and Pets

Pets have played a host of crucial roles in war, from boosting the morale of soldiers to helping rescue lost soldiers behind enemy lines. Their importance is borne out by the huge numbers of animals used – in the First World War alone an estimated sixteen million animals were used by belligerents on both sides, including horses, dogs, mules, pigeons, oxen, camels, elephants, cats, goats and even geese. Their bravery was outstanding, and many were killed or injured for their efforts. Yet all the animals featured here were originally pets, donated by their owners to help the war effort, and in many cases were returned to their owners after war ended to resume being pets. What makes these animals so extraordinary is how well they adapted from a life of domestic calm to hostile environments on the battlefield or deep inside enemy territory.

Some of these animals were decorated with military awards for bravery and in the Second World War a unique military award was instituted by Maria Dickin, the founder of the People's Dispensary for Sick Animals. It was called the Dickin Medal, often dubbed the 'animal's Victoria Cross', and became the highest British award for bravery an animal could win during the war. Only fifty-three Dickin Medals were awarded, and such is their rarity that they are now one of the most valued military medals, fetching tens of thousands of pounds at auction in recent years. The most recent price for a Dickin Medal at auction at the time of going to press was £23,000.

These, then, are just a few of the many heroic stories of individual pet bravery in warfare, in some cases rewarded with the highest honours. They show qualities demonstrated by animals throughout *Pet Heroes* and make a fitting climax to the whole notion of animal intelligence, bravery, loyalty, navigation and endurance.

* * *

DOGS

Dogs truly made their mark in the First World War. Thanks to their loyalty and intelligence, low physical profile and fast legs, they could run over the battlefield's most hostile territory, between trenches and over no-man's land. They were used for an astonishing range of jobs: pulling machine guns, carrying ammunition, laying telephone cables from rolls strapped on to their backs, locating wounded soldiers on the battlefield, running messages in pouches hung on their collars, keeping away rats and even pulling supplies over the Alps for the Italian army. These were difficult tasks because they were dangerous and because many dogs couldn't stay calm under gunfire and artillery barrages, or didn't have the discipline to resist food and petting from soldiers during an errand.

The dogs that were successfully trained often became so good at their jobs that the enemy targeted them as dangerous opponents, and particularly so with messenger dogs. These dogs could navigate journeys up to a few miles long often over difficult muddy craters, carrying a message fixed in a wallet to their collar. They moved swiftly and silently and were often the only means of moving information across the front line trenches when telephone lines had been cut and no other lines of communication were possible.

STUBBY

One of the most famous First World War dog heroes was Stubby, a stray pit bull terrier originally picked up from the streets of

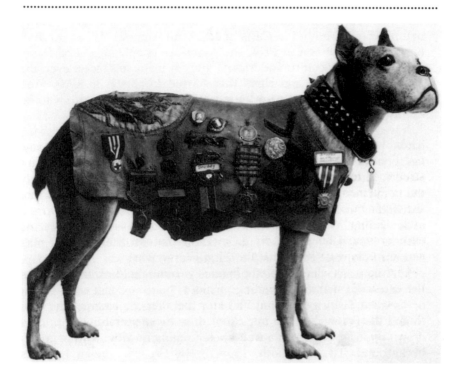

Stubby was America's most famous First World War hero dog, whose bravery eventually earnt him introductions to no less than three American presidents. (Smithsonian Institute, Washington DC)

Hartford, Connecticut by Robert Conroy. Stubby became so well known for his war exploits that he was introduced over the years to three successive American presidents.

Stubby was smuggled to the American front lines in 1918 by Conroy and became the mascot of the 102nd Infantry, earning his keep by doing sentry work and searching no-man's land for the wounded, lying next to them so that rescue squads could find them. But his exploits also included a number of high dramas. One night while the troops slept he warned of an impending gas attack in time for the soldiers to get their gas masks on. Another time he sank his teeth into a German who had infiltrated the American lines. Word of Stubby's daredevil exploits swept the front lines and he was dubbed the 'Hero Dog'. He was presented with awards for gallantry, so many in fact that he had to have a special blanket made for him to pin all his medals on.

By the end of the war Stubby had survived seventeen battles with his company and when he returned home he was greeted as a national hero, and was introduced to President Woodrow Wilson. He then spent his days touring the country with Robert Conroy raising money for war veterans. Such was his enduring fame that in 1921 Robert Conroy and Stubby met with President Harding, and in 1925 President Coolidge welcomed the pair at the White House.

CHIPS

In the Second World War, dogs were used in even more audacious roles. One of the most famous American war dogs was Chips, a mixed-breed German shepherd, husky and collie, used by the 3rd Infantry for guard work. But Chips really came into his own under battle. When the 3rd Infantry Division landed in Sicily at daybreak on 10 July 1943, as part of the Allied invasion of Italy, Chips and his handler, John Rowell, found themselves and the other soldiers pinned down on their beachhead by machine-gun fire. About 300 yards ahead they saw what appeared to be a small grass-covered hut, in fact a camouflaged pillbox from which the gunfire was coming. The Americans could do nothing but lie flat on the sand. Suddenly, without any command, Chips broke loose and ran towards the hut, jumping into it through the gun slit. Moments later the firing stopped and an Italian soldier appeared with Chips biting at his arm and throat, with three other Italian soldiers following behind. All four surrendered to Rowell. Chips had put up a considerable fight inside the pillbox, and suffered scalp wounds and powder burns from gunfire.

Yet his exploits that day were not over. Later that night, Chips alerted his company to a group of approaching Italian soldiers. Rowell ambushed them and took all ten Italians prisoner. The reputation of Chips spread rapidly through the division and news of his feats was flashed back to the US where the press titled him a 'hero dog'. Chips was congratulated in two speeches in Congress and in Italy was introduced to General Eisenhower. However, Chips got a little too familiar with the Supreme Commander of the Allied Forces and nipped his hand when he tried to pat him. Two months later he was awarded the Distinguished Service Cross, and soon after that the Silver Star and the Purple Heart, the only dog in history to receive such top medals despite regulations forbidding medals being issued to animals. Unfortunately one military commander protested that giving these prestigious medals to animals denigrated the awards and Chips's decorations were withdrawn. Nevertheless, there was no doubting that Chips was an heroic dog whose exploits made history.

A dog's powerful sense of smell has been one of its most treasured skills in war. Dogs like Alsatians were sometimes the only way to reveal the enemy hidden in jungles or underground bunkers and tunnels. It was a particularly skilful job for the dogs because they had to hunt the scent as quietly as possible and, when they had found the enemy, give a silent signal to the handler, such as lying down on the ground, when the natural instinct of most dogs would be to bark. Those dogs which could be trained to be silent trackers proved so successful they struck fear into the enemy. In the Second World War, the Japanese came to hate the dogs used by the Americans for searching them out in jungles on the other side of the Pacific, and in the Vietnam War the Americans again used dogs to devastating effect against the elaborate underground shelters used by the Vietcong.

Another vital and deadly role for specially trained sniffer dogs was searching out landmines. They had to track down the explosives hidden underground and sit down the instant they picked up the smell so that the mine could be located. Mine dogs were highly valued because they were more effective than metal detectors and they were usually the only way of detecting mines made of plastic or wood. They could also recognise earth that had been recently dug up, which could indicate a mine below. These mine dogs were especially important in clearing paths during the Normandy D-Day invasion in 1944, and for several months they worked every day making safe the Allies' advance through western Europe.

RICKY

One of the most astonishing mine dogs was a Welsh sheepdog called Ricky. As the Allies were pushing through Holland towards the Rhine, they were hampered by minefields laid by the retreating Germans. Ricky was clearing a canal bank in Holland when an undetected mine blew up three feet from him, killing the squad's commander and wounding Ricky. But with astonishing bravery he continued searching for mines and pinpointed several more before collapsing from his wounds. He was awarded a Dickin Medal.

BEAUTY

The sniffing skills of dogs were also put to use on the home front during the London Blitz, searching out survivors buried in the debris of bombing raids. The remains of buildings were often highly dangerous, gas leaks and broken glass were common hazards, and buried survivors often unable to make any noise. Yet at the onset of the Blitz the civil defence authorities believed that dogs would be no use because the mass of different smells at a bomb site would distract them. They were proved very wrong.

The breakthrough in using sniffer dogs started with Beauty. She belonged to Bill Barnet, a leader of one of the many rescue squads that searched wreckage for lost animals, and accompanied him on his searches purely to keep him company. It was entirely on her own initiative that she started life-saving, when one night in 1940 she wandered off and started digging intensively on her own. The rescue workers realised she had found something and they discovered a cat trapped and still alive. From that small beginning, Beauty became the pioneer of rescue dogs, searching out human as well as animal casualties in bomb runs. She was awarded the Peoples' Dispensary for Sick Animals' Pioneer Medal, usually only given to humans.

RIP

Hot on the heels of Beauty's pioneering work came Rip, a homeless stray adopted by Mr E. King, who worked in a Civil Defence unit

Sheepdog Ricky helped spearhead the Allies' advance through occupied Europe in the Second World War by detecting landmines. Even when he was badly injured by a mine explosion he continued working, and was awarded the prestigious Dickin Medal. (People's Dispensary for Sick Animals)

in the London dock area. Rip made himself indispensable by voluntarily digging through rubble for survivors, as Mr King explained: 'When I came across Rip sniffing around on the job, I always knew there was someone trapped in the ruins.'

IRMA AND PSYCHE

The success of Beauty and Rip was the turning point in using dogs for rescue missions, and from then on dogs were specially trained to search out survivors in the wreckage of London. Two of the most successful search dogs were a pair of Alsatians, Irma and Psyche, belonging to Margaret Griffin. Between them they located a total of 233 people during the war. One example of their work happened on 5 February 1945 at 2.30 a.m. in Chingford, Essex where a rocket had gone right through a house. Despite the heavy smell of escaping gas, Irma scrabbled around a buried bath and, as Margaret cleared away some of the debris, she discovered a cavity where a baby's cry could be heard. Digging deeper the search party found a woman with a little boy and baby trapped in a small bomb shelter under the rubble. About an hour later the rescue squad leader suggested the search was over and the dogs could go home, but Psyche insisted on lying down to indicate more survivors and, after the workers dug four feet deeper, they discovered the father of the family still alive.

In all, five Blitz search dogs won Dickin Medals, and their success helped create dog search teams for use in peacetime after the war, finding survivors of earthquakes, floods and other civilian disasters.

ROB THE 'PARADOG'

Many dogs in the Second World War were used for far less dangerous tasks, such as guarding supplies or prisoners of war. But one guard dog was so intelligent that he was drafted into top secret missions deep inside enemy territory, and even now some of his ventures are shrouded in mystery.

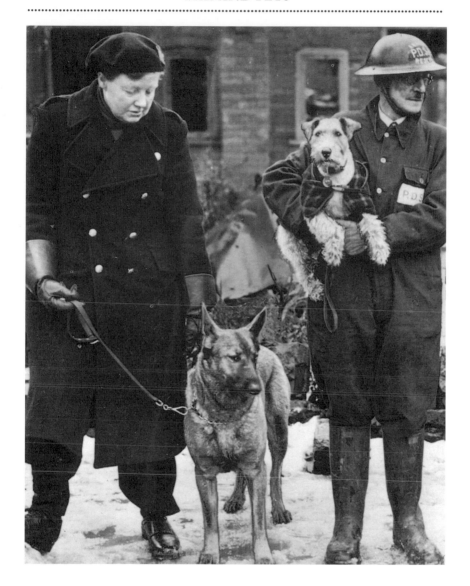

Irma, the Alsatian, located a record total of 191 buried people during the London Blitz in the Second World War, although at the start of the bombing dogs were thought by the authorities incapable of helping rescue efforts. (Imperial War Museum)

Rob, the parachuting collie, receiving the Dickin Medal for Gallantry.
(Imperial War Museum)

Rob the 'Paradog' was a parachuting agent used by the Special Air Service (SAS) behind enemy lines to patrol and guard small groups of commandoes. He was probably the most decorated animal in British history, winning eight medals including the Dickin Medal, but for a long time Rob's exploits remained a top secret. It took a good deal of research by Evelyn Le Chêne in her book *Silent Heroes* (1994) to bring Rob's war record to light.

Rob was a collie originally brought up in the countryside before being donated to the army. He started military life as a guard dog stationed with the SAS in Tunisia under the command of quartermaster Tom Burt, who recognised the dog's intelligence by his ability to pick out thieves from friends in an epidemic of pilfering from the army's stores. At Burt's suggestion Rob was tested for parachute jumping and made several successful jumps and – most unusually for a dog – without making any noise. In fact, Rob seemed to enjoy his parachuting and on command he would jump from the aircraft, a special trigger opening his parachute, and he would lie still on the ground until his handler joined him. He was then trained to round up his patrol in darkness or daylight.

Rob made over twenty solo parachute drops, including at least two in Italy hundreds of miles deep into German-held territory. His first mission there is thought to have been a drop with Lieutenant Alastair McGregor and Private McQueen into Chieti. After the Italian surrender in September 1943, masses of Allied prisoners of war were released from Italian camps and Rob and the SAS had to get them back to Allied lines as the German forces advanced rapidly to occupy the country. Often in extreme danger, Rob helped escort the freed prisoners to Chieti, where the 8th Army was expected to arrive by 20 October. But the army failed to rendezvous on time and McGregor and McQueen had to fight a pitch battle with a detachment of Germans until they could slip away. After four months on the run with Rob acting as lookout against the enemy, they managed to get back to British lines where they discovered that all of them had been posted missing in action.

By January 1944 almost the whole of Italy was under German occupation and the Allies planned an audacious amphibious assault on Anzio, well behind German lines, to break through to Rome and northern Italy. To make the landings safe the Allies had to destroy German reconnaissance aircraft based at San Egidio, and Rob was despatched with a six-man SAS team on 12 January 1944 to blow the planes up. Although the airbase was heavily defended, the SAS patrol got through and bombed all seven planes on the base, but as they escaped they were caught in a blast which killed one officer and severely wounded another. Rob led the survivors back to base, acting as lookout for German search parties and successfully leading them back to safety on 24 January. On 8 February 1945, at a packed ceremony covered by the BBC and the press, Rob received the Dickin Medal from Major Philip Sydney, VC.

RIN-TIN-TIN

Dogs have also served a vital role in war by raising the morale of soldiers and bringing them a reminder of home. Against army regulations, soldiers in the First World War often adopted dogs as pets for friendship, and by far the best known dog eventually became a Hollywood star. Rin-Tin-Tin was originally born in a German trench but was abandoned by his mother during an American attack. He was found alone by an American officer, Lieutenant Lee Duncan, who named him after the good-luck dolls French girls gave to soldiers. Duncan looked after him with the 135th Aero Squadron throughout puppyhood and trained the dog to do tricks. After the war he auditioned Rin-Tin-Tin for a Hollywood film, and the dog became such a huge star in the silent movies that for several years he was Warner Brothers' major source of revenue and was given top billing over his human co-stars. His success continued into the talkies era until his death in 1932 at the grand age of sixteen years old.

JUDY

The most famous morale-boosting dog of the Second World War was Judy, probably the only pet recognised as an official prisoner of war and who became a British legend. She was originally the mascot of HMS *Grasshopper* in the Far East, but in February 1942 the ship was bombed off the coast of Sumatra in Indonesia and Judy and the crew were left marooned on a small tropical island. The prospects for survival looked bleak and death from thirst seemed inevitable until Judy found a fresh water spring that had been buried under high tide on the shore.

The crew were rescued by a passing Chinese junk, which took them to Sumatra from where they attempted to trek across the island on foot. But they were surrounded by the Japanese and all, including Judy, were taken prisoner and sent to a prison camp in Medan in the north of the island. There Judy was looked after by Leading Aircraftman Frank Williams of the RAF who shared his

Judy was probably the only animal registered as a Japanese prisoner of war, suffering appalling hardships but loyally guarding her men and raising their morale. (Fox Photos Ltd)

meagre rice ration with her and persuaded the Japanese Commandant to register her as a prisoner of war.

In return, Judy acted as lookout for dangerous animals – even suffering a scar from a fight with an alligator – and helped raise the morale of the prisoners. In June 1944 the POWs were shipped from Sumatra to Singapore, but she wasn't allowed to go. So Williams smuggled her aboard the transport ship inside a rice sack where she kept totally silent. The next day the ship was struck by two torpedoes and both Williams and Judy survived two hours in the sea before being picked up and sent to another prison camp in Medan, where the same Commandant they had suffered before condemned her to death. Williams found a safe hiding place for her and not long afterwards the camp was liberated by the British. Williams again smuggled Judy aboard ship, and returned her safely back to England where she became front page news and was awarded the Dickin Medal for bravery and endurance. On 8 June 1946, Judy's bark was broadcast live on world radio when she contributed to a special BBC Victory Day celebration.

* * *

CATS

During the First World War, cats were vital in keeping up morale in the nightmare conditions of the trenches and often earned their keep by catching mice. But it was not until just after the Second World War that a cat was officially decorated for bravery.

SIMON

During the Chinese Civil War in 1949, Chiang Kai-shek's pro-Western Nationalists were losing heavily to the Communists. The Royal Navy sent the frigate HMS *Amethyst* up the Yangtze River to Shanghai to relieve a destroyer guarding the British Consulate there. But as the *Amethyst* sailed upriver Communist guns on the shore opened fire and the ship was hit fifty-four times before running aground on a sandbank. On board the ship were 145 crew and the ship's cat Simon. Forty-six men were killed in the attack and Simon was hurled back from a blast less than three feet away from him which left him badly singed and bleeding from shrapnel wounds.

The attack on the *Amethyst* provoked worldwide outrage and although no further attacks were launched the ship remained aground in a political limbo in stifling heat, plagued by insects, food and water rationed and infested with rats. The surviving crew nursed Simon back to health and, despite his pain, he went back to work a few days later catching rats. Even more than that, the survivors spoke of the enormous sense of normality Simon brought to the entire ship during three months of tense stalemate. Eventually the crew grew so desperate to escape they made a perilous break for the sea 140 miles downriver. On 30 July, on a high tide and under cover of darkness, the ship started up and broke free, running the gauntlet of shore batteries. Incredibly, several hours later, it had managed to escape to safe waters. When the *Amethyst* arrived back in Plymouth in October 1949 she was given a heroes' welcome and Simon was made famous, his picture appearing in newspapers all over the world. Sadly, the strain of injury and trauma on Simon was too great and he died shortly afterwards, but he was awarded the Dickin Medal posthumously.

* * *

PIGEONS

At first it seems a bizarre idea that birds could ever reach the heights of heroism scaled by cats and dogs. Many gave comfort as pets, like cages of canaries used for brightening up field hospital wards and even on hospital trains (although they were probably more useful in giving early warning of gas attacks). The American marines in the Pacific War even had a duck called Siwash as their mascot, who survived three major naval battles and led the invasion of Tarawa with flapping wings, outstretched neck and much quacking.

Yet the unsung heroes of the war birds were pigeons. In the First World War, some 100,000 pigeons were used by the British to fly urgent messages. Their flights were heroic, saving countless lives by running messages when there was often no other means of communication. An advancing tank, for instance, had no alternative way to report its progress, and pigeons were even liberated from planes flying at up to 100 miles per hour to report on the battlefield below. What makes their bravery even more remarkable is that pigeons – unlike dogs, horses, mules and the other war animals – cannot be trained for warfare. They were all racing pigeons volunteered by dedicated pigeon fanciers, and had had no previous experience of artillery, gunfire and all the other hazards of flying through hostile airspace. For these reasons they were the most decorated animals in both world wars, and of the fifty-three Dickin Medals awarded in total in the Second World War, pigeons received thirty-one of them.

In the First World War, pigeons scored a number of advantages over other animal messengers. They were faster than dogs and less likely to be shot, flying at 300–500 feet. But they still suffered a huge number of fatalities from stray bullets, exploding artillery shells, gas attacks, birds of prey set on them by the enemy and bad weather.

They were put to some ingenious uses. The Intelligence Corps dropped pigeons into enemy-held Belgium and France in baskets with messages asking the civilian population to supply intelligence information. The Germans became so alarmed they posted notices threatening to shoot anyone caught returning a pigeon with a message. The Army Pigeon Service dropped a total of 16,554 pigeons singly by parachute into enemy-held Europe with questionnaires for the finders to send back to Britain with information about the Germans. The pigeons sustained heavy losses on these missions – many birds were not found or were discovered by the enemy or collaborators, and only 1,842 returned to the UK. The Germans even had a special corps equipped with falcons and hawks in the Pas de Calais area to hunt down the pigeons on their flight back to England.

The Germans also tried sabotaging pigeon carriers by substituting Ally birds with one of their own so that anyone stupid enough to send back a message with their name or address on it could then be traced. But the Allies, in turn, sent the Germans bogus messages using pigeons carrying imitation message capsules. They were also used for passing information from agents and SAS squads operating in enemy territory, and for sending news to and from MI9 (the Escape Service that organised escape chains for downed Allied airmen and escapees from prisoner of war camps).

On the battlefront, a good example of the value of pigeons is the Battle of the Somme in 1916, in which the French alone used 5,000 pigeons of which only two per cent failed to return despite the intense shell-fire and often poor weather conditions. A 'normal' day was 25 September 1916: 'It was a typical September day, and good for flying, but the artillery preparation was deafening, and tested the birds to the limit. Messages began to come in from 2p.m., and the regularity with which the birds homed and with which the advance could be followed was quite remarkable.' (From Major Alec Waley, O.C. Carrier Pigeon Service on the French front, quoted in A. H. Osman, *Pigeons in the Great War*, 1929.)

VERDUN PIGEON AND DOG

One of the most dramatic rescue missions by a pigeon helped save the battle for Verdun. The small town of Verdun was held by only a few hundred French troops from February to April 1916. The Germans were determined to take the town, and launched a continuous artillery barrage, while the French were equally determined to defend Verdun at all costs, even though they were running short of ammunition and supplies. Even more worrying, all their telephone lines were destroyed and when their last pigeon and messenger dog were killed they were left without any communication with the outside world. Their only hope lay three miles away where French forces held a black greyhound called Satan, whose handler, a soldier called Duvalle, was trapped inside Verdun. By releasing Satan, the French headquarters hoped he would run to Duvalle and carry a message pleading with the garrison to hold out as relief was being sent, and take with him a package of two pigeons to bring back a reply.

The dog ran through a hail of bullets to find Duvalle, but by the time he reached him with his vital message he was seriously wounded. The French defenders released the carrier pigeons with duplicate messages giving details of the attacking German battery. One pigeon was killed outright but, despite being badly wounded, the other got through to headquarters. Soon after, the supporting French artillery opened up and silenced the German guns. The pigeon died but was posthumously awarded the highest French decoration for valour in war, the *Légion d'Honneur*.

GI JOE

Despite the technological advances of the Second World War, nearly 200,000 young pigeons were donated to the services and proved even more versatile for the Allies than in the previous world war. Of the pigeons decorated for bravery most were mainly used for running messages for the military services. For example, on 18 October 1943 a company of the British 56th Division fighting in Italy unexpectedly broke through German positions and captured the town of Colvi Vacchia. Unfortunately, British 10th Corps headquarters were just about to bomb Colvi to help break the German positions, and the planes were already warming up on schedule to take off at 11.10 a.m. The officers in Colvi tried calling back to HQ to call off the attack but the phones to the airfield were dead and radio units weren't working. They only had twenty-five minutes left before the bombing raid started, inadvertently putting over a hundred Allied soldiers' lives at risk.

The only way headquarters in Colvi could get a message through to cancel the bombing mission was by using GI Joe, a US pigeon messenger. The air was alive with gunfire, yet GI Joe made the

Carrier pigeons were often the only way of sending messages in both world wars. GI Joe was a pigeon who helped save a hundred Allied soldiers' lives by preventing a bombing mission by their own side, and he was later awarded the Dickin Medal for animal heroism. (People's Dispensary for Sick Animals)

twenty-mile journey and reached the airfield with five minutes to spare, just as the planes were preparing to take off. The mission was called off and the British soldiers in Colvi were spared.

After the war, GI Joe was flown from the US to England and taken to the Tower of London, where he was received by military and diplomatic officials with a guard of honour formed by Beefeaters, the tower guards. Major General Charles Keightley, commander of the 56th Division, hung a Dickin Medal around Joe's neck. 'I'm proud of you, Joe,' General Keightley said.

WINKIE

RAF bomber crews routinely carried a messenger pigeon in a basket in case they were forced to ditch without radio contact. One of the best known pigeon rescuers was Winkie, a hen pigeon. On 23 February 1942 she was on board a Beaufort bomber returning from a strike off the Norwegian coast when the plane developed engine trouble and was forced to ditch 120 miles off the Scottish coast. During impact the pigeon escaped from her container and fell into the oily sea before struggling clear. She took off at 4 p.m., while the crew of four floated on a rubber dinghy. The pigeon then flew 129 miles to her RAF base, arriving there soon after dawn the next morning, exhausted, wet and oily.

The air search for the crew had been on a very poor radio fix and up until then unsuccessful. Even though the pigeon arrived without a message, Sergeant Davidson of the RAF Pigeon Service calculated the position of the ditched plane from the condition of the pigeon, the direction it flew from and the hours of daylight available, and re-directed the search to a new area. Soon afterwards the crew was located and rescued, the first rescue during the Second World War attributed to a pigeon. That night the crew gave a dinner in her honour.

Incidentally, they christened her 'Winkie' because she appeared to be winking at them – in fact, she was blinking slowly because she was so tired!

PIGEON DD.43.Q.879

The Australians had their own outstanding military success with pigeons. During the fight for Manus Island in New Guinea, the 1st Marines sent a patrol to the village of Dravito to scout out the Japanese strength. There they saw preparations for an imminent attack, but on returning to base with the information they were ambushed by the Japanese. The patrol's radio was knocked out and two carrier pigeons were shot down. The only way of getting an SOS message through was to release their last carrier pigeon, codenamed DD.43.Q.879, and despite heavy gunfire it reached headquarters thirty miles away in forty-six minutes. As a result, the Australian marines launched a bombing raid on the Japanese, the patrol escaped back to base and the large attack was thwarted.

KENNY LASS

The Resistance groups in Occupied Europe also turned to pigeon carriers for help. Radio operators in these Resistance groups were continually at risk from detection by the enemy and pigeons were often the only way for messages to be safely sent back to Britain. They carried vital information, such as requests for supplies of weapons and explosives for sabotage work and to coordinate their air drops, enemy movements and positions such as the locations of rocket sites used for bombing southern England.

Kenny Lass was the first pigeon used for this secret line of communication. She was first dropped with an agent by parachute into occupied France and was hidden for eleven days in a safehouse before the agent was ready to write out a message and release the pigeon on 20 October 1940. She arrived back in Kenley, England over 300 miles away in six hours and forty minutes. She returned again to France the following year on exactly the same type of secret mission.

MARY OF EXETER

Possibly one of the bravest of all pigeons was Mary of Exeter. She once went missing for four days after a mission in Europe, but arrived back with her message intact but with her neck and right breast badly slashed, evidently attacked by a hawk. Two months later she had recovered and then returned from another mission with part of her wing shot away and three pellets in her body. During air raids on her home loft in Exeter, a bomb fell close to her loft killing most of her fellow pigeons, but she survived. After recuperation she returned again to active service and, following another mission, was picked up almost dead in a field, wounded virtually all over her body and completely exhausted. She was awarded the Dickin Medal for outstanding endurance.

8

Everyday Heroes

Pets are much more than public heroes. There are an estimated twenty-six million dogs and twenty-three million cats in western Europe, and forty-eight million dogs and twenty-seven million cats in the US. In an everyday, humdrum, domestic situation these pets have been proved to be good for our health and, in my estimation, that makes them heroic in a private sort of way. Simply stroking a furry pet helps reduce an owner's stress, and just being in the presence of a friendly animal tends to make both adults and children more relaxed, regardless if they are stroking them or not. Scientists have found that people owning pets have slightly lower cholesterol levels and blood pressure than non-owners. And it's been proven that anyone watching an aquarium full of tropical fish experiences a fall in blood pressure.

James Serpell at the University of Pennsylvania has made lengthy investigations on pet ownership and believes that one way pets can improve a person's health is by giving a special sort of emotional support that is less common than in relationships between people. It seems that pets improve the social life of their owners – people walking their dogs in a park are more likely to have positive social encounters with other people. Also, pet owners tend to have greater emotional empathy towards other people as well as animals.

Pets provide even more striking benefits to patients living an isolated life or convalescing from a heart attack – these people are slightly more likely to survive if they have a pet, no matter what sort of animal it is. This is nothing to do with the psychology of the pet owner, or the severity of the heart attack. It's a definite effect of the pet itself, and it's such a clearcut effect that if all the heart attack victims in America owned a pet it would help save an estimated 30,000 lives annually of more than a million Americans who die of heart disease every year.

Mental wellbeing also improves from having pets around. They help withdrawn children who are afraid to communicate make rapid progress, and many disturbed children with a history of violence or drug abuse have been shown to grow in self-esteem with animals, which in turn greatly improves their behaviour with people. Adult psychiatric patients also respond well to pets, even those patients who have failed with other, more orthodox treatments.

These results have been translated into practical use. More than half of all nursing homes, clinics and hospitals in the US use animals for therapy, and resident dogs and cats in nursing homes for the elderly are becoming more common in Britain. There is also a unique pet visiting scheme in Britain called the Pro-Dogs Active Therapy scheme, known as PAT Dogs, which has some 4,000 registered dogs, and arranges for their volunteer owners to take their pets to visit hospitals, hospices, old age homes and other health institutions.

Quite apart from the benefits to health, pets have other virtues, and some breeds of dogs can make excellent guards. Brian Leonard of the Kennel Club in Britain favours Chihuahuas – he owns one and has never been burgled. 'It makes more sense to choose a breed with a bark that sounds like a bigger dog, but which is easier to feed and look after, and will fit into the lifestyle of the modern family,' he says. This is where the smaller, territorial breeds with their big voices come into their own, because they are vociferous, wary of unusual noises and defensive of their home territory. The guiding principle is to choose a breed whose natural instinct is protection but not aggression.

Intelligent dogs build up a perception of regular happenings in the home, so that anything out of the ordinary – such as the arrival of an intruder – will cause them to bark and defend their territory. Dog behaviourists believe, for example, that the reason so many postmen get bitten is because, each day, it appears to the dog that this stranger is trying to break into the home: people never signal this is a friendly caller by greeting him or her. Yorkshire terriers and Jack Russells are recommended burglar deterrents.

But what do pets get from their owners? Obviously they get a home and food, but the numbers of abandoned pets during summer and Christmas holidays show how temporary their welcome can be. The converse of abandoned pets is also very real – 'pet burnout' is a phenomenon with symptoms of tiredness and irritability in pets which has been recorded among some dogs and cats acting as therapists to the ill or deprived. Similar problems can also arise in ordinary domestic homes where pets don't get enough privacy. It seems that pets need their own private lives. In some ways humans get more out of their pets than vice versa.

CONCLUSION

Perhaps the stories in this book all seem a million miles away from the contented cat curled up on your lap, or the excited dog running around chasing a ball. Fortunately most pets won't have to face the extreme dangers that put their character to the test, but many of those who have been exposed to perils have shown great heroism and in so many different ways. They have saved us from accidents, criminals, medical emergencies, natural disasters, helped to fight wars and much more. In the thousands of years of living with humans they've formed such close bonds they look on us as their leaders, which partly explains much of their loyalty and why they risk their lives for us. But pet heroics go far beyond an animal's instincts.

They have used great ingenuity in saving life – what psychologists call problem-solving intelligence. There are sides to their behaviour we simply don't fully understand. Their memory seems to be almost photographic. They seem to read our moods, behaviour and health. Some people say they can read our minds as well. What we can say for sure is that they have powers of awareness which seem to defy conventional science.

There is a natural temptation to treat pets as if they were human, but I believe they are very different. They live in a world dominated by smell, hearing and sight, much better than our senses, although they have a poor sense of colour. They probably have other senses we are oblivious to, such as feeling air pressure, magnetism and electricity.

But do pets think about their lives, can they empathise with humans, do they plan what they are going to do tomorrow morning, do they have a conscience and morals? These are questions many animal behaviourists call 'theory of mind' and their answer is no. They say that cats and dogs only have the level of understanding roughly equivalent to a toddler. They also say that the most intelligent animals, chimpanzees and gorillas, have the mind of about a four-and-a-half-year-old child – which, incidentally, is the critical stage in human development when we show all the signs of having a mind with self-consciousness. So although pets are not humans on four legs they are wonderful creatures. They show us the affection we crave, they defer to us and they never speak back to us. They are our guardians. And there are many mysteries about them we have yet to fathom. Pets are indeed heroes.

REFERENCES

Arnold, Edwin, *The Soul of the Beast* (London: Macmillan, 1960).

Bardens, Dennis, *Psychic Animals* (London: Hale, 1987).

Burton, Maurice, *The Sixth Sense of Animals* (London: Dent, 1973).

—— *Just Like an Animal* (London: Dent, 1978).

Cooper, Jilly, *Animals in War* (London: William Heinemann, 1983).

Coren, Stanley, *The Intelligence of Dogs, Canine Consciousness and Capabilities* (London: Headline, 1994).

Duncan, Lee, *The Rin-Tin-Tin Book of Dog Care* (New Jersey: Prentice-Hall, 1958).

Finlay, Wilfred & Hancock, Gillian, *Clever and Courageous Dogs* (London: Kaye & Wood, 1978).

Fox, Michael W., *Understanding Your Dog* (London: Blond & Briggs, 1972).

—— *Understanding Your Cat* (London: Blond & Briggs, 1974).

Gaddis, Vincent & Gaddis, Margaret, *The Strange World of Animals and Pets* (New York: Cowles, 1970).

Gilroy, James, *Furred and Feathered Heroes of World War II* (London: Trafalgar, 1946).

Greene, David, *Incredible Cats* (London: Methuen, 1984).

Harpur, Merrily, *Pig Overboard! And Other Strange But True Letters to the Field* (London: Robson Books, 1984).

Heim, Alice, *Barking Up The Right Tree, or, Intelligence and Personality in Dogs* (London: Pelham Books, 1980).

Ingledew, E., *True Stories About Animals and Birds* (Devon: Stockwell, 1981).

Johnson, Sally P., *Everyman's Ark* (London: Hamish Hamilton, 1962).

Le Chêne, Evelyn, *Silent Heroes* (London: Souvenir Press, 1994).

Lemish, Michael G., *War Dogs. Canines in Combat* (Washington: Brassey's, 1996).

Lewis, Martyn, *Cats in the News* (London: Macdonald, 1991).

—— *Dogs in the News* (London: Little Brown, 1992).

Mitchell, John & Rickard, R. J. M., *Living Wonders* (London: Thames & Hudson, 1982).

Osman, A. H., *Pigeons in the Great War* (London: The Racing Pigeon Publishing Company, 1929).

Osman, W. H., *Pigeons in World War II* (London: The Racing Pigeon Publishing Company, 1950).

Roberts, Yvonne, *Animal Heroes* (Oxford: Pelham Books, 1990).

St Hill Bourne, Dorothea, *They Also Serve* (Winchester: Winchester Publications, 1957).

Schul, Bill, *Psychic Powers of Animals* (London: Coronet, 1978).

Scott-Ordish, Lesley, *Heroic Dogs* (London: Arlington Books, 1990).

Serpell, James, *In the Company of Animals, a Study of Human-Animal Relationships* (Oxford: Blackwells, 1986).

Shaw, Peter, *Animal War Heroes* (London: A & C Black, 1933).

Sheldrake, Rupert, *Seven Experiments That Could Change The World* (London: Fourth Estate, 1994).

Steiger, Brad & Steiger, Sherry Hansen, *Strange Powers of Pets* (London: Headline, 1993).

ACKNOWLEDGEMENTS

I would very much like to thank all the following for their magnificent help in providing information:

Nick Southall and colleagues at the National Canine Defence League; Lesley Scott-Ordish at PRO Dogs; Sara Powell and Isabelle George at the People's Dispensary for Sick Animals headquarters; Jo Crozier and Sue Atkinson at the Royal Society for the Protection of Animals headquarters; Pam Smart; Glen Ford at the UK Geological Survey, Edinburgh; the Plymouth *Herald*; *Cat Fancy* magazine; Betty Lewis and Joyce Briggs at the American Humane Association; Melissa Bassett at the Massachusetts Society for Prevention of Cruelty to Animals; North Shore Animal League, New York; Sue Swanwick at the Society for Prevention of Cruelty to Animals, Ontario; Amy White at the Toronto Humane Society; Karen Kohera and Dave Corner at the Ralston-Perina Hall of Fame; the Royal New Zealand Society for Prevention of Cruelty to Animals; *Australian Women's Weekly*; Stephanie Dorezas at the Humane Society of the US; John Janzen at the Society for Prevention of Cruelty to Animals, Alberta; the Society for Prevention of Cruelty to Animals, National Council of Southern Africa; the staff of the British Library, British Museum, London.